WHERE DO WE GO FROM HERE

Twilight and evening bell,
And after that the dark!
And may there be no sadness of farewell,
When I embark;
For, tho' from out our bourne of time and place
The flood may bear me far,
I hope to see my Pilot face to face
When I have crossed the bar.

Tennyson

Where Do We Go From Here?

The Case for Life beyond Death

David Winter

Hodder & Stoughton
LONDON SYDNEY AUCKLAND

Biblical quotations are from
the New International Version unless otherwise indicated.

Copyright © 1996 by David Winter

First published in Great Britain 1996

The right of David Winter to be identified as the Author of
the Work has been asserted by him in accordance with the
Copyright, Designs and Patents Act 1988.

10 9 8 7 6 5 4 3 2 1

British Library Cataloguing in Publication Data
A record for this book is available from the British Library

ISBN 0 340 65635 2

Typeset by Hewer Text Composition Services, Edinburgh
Printed and bound in Great Britain by
Cox and Wyman Ltd, Reading, Berkshire

Hodder and Stoughton Ltd
A Division of Hodder Headline PLC
338 Euston Road
London NW1 3BH

CONTENTS

Introduction   ix

1 Thinking about Death   1
2 'What Happens When I Die?'   7
3 Self, Spirit, Soul   13
4 Evidence for Survival   25
5 The Resurrection of Jesus   41
6 What Kind of Body?   51
7 What is Heaven Like?   65
8 Who Goes There?   75

   Appendix I   91
   Appendix II   97
   Appendix III   99

ABOUT THIS BOOK

This book is not a theological or academic thesis, but an attempt to present the general reader with the Christian case for life beyond death. It's meant to be read rather than studied, so I have not littered the text with footnotes, biblical references and so on. But at the same time I appreciate that if it is to present a *case* it must offer not only my advocacy but also the evidence of the witnesses. So at the end of the book I set out in three appendices the Bible passages on which I have based my case, the details of the books and other writings cited and a list of books for suggested further reading. In that way I hope that this book will meet two needs – for a readable presentation of the arguments for life after death, and (for those who want it) some resources for further study and exploration of the subject.

INTRODUCTION

In the early 1970s I wrote a book called *Hereafter*. As you might guess from the title, it was about life beyond death. Perhaps because there weren't many books on the subject, or perhaps because it struck a chord in the decade that thought it had invented the word 'spiritual', it became a religious bestseller – not only in Britain, but literally across the world.

Much has changed since then. Technology has roared ahead. There has been a major world recession, with its victims scattered across every continent. And almost every week, it seems, there is news of fresh scientific discovery. Technically, communication has advanced enormously, through computer, modem and internet. We feel as though we know everything. 'Spirituality' has given way, as the buzz-word, to cybernetics.

And yet the suspicion remains that in fact we know nothing. We can 'communicate', in the sense that we can convey information at the speed of light across the planet, but for many people the communication that really matters has got stuck in the machinery.

The great word of the close of the millenium is 'breakdown'. Families break down, relationships break down, communities break down. We are tremendously successful at things that don't matter very much, and apparently increasingly hopeless at things that truly shape our lives and determine our well-being. It sometimes seems that we always know the answer to the question 'How?', but struggle to give any response to the question 'Why?' In other words, we suffer from an acute shortage of *meaning*.

'There is darkness without, and when I die there will be darkness within,' wrote philosopher Bertrand Russell just before his death. 'There is no splendour, no vastness anywhere; only triviality for a moment, and then nothing.' He wrote that in the late 1960s, but it captures with almost eerie accuracy the mood of the turn of the century. It seems as though humankind has finally fallen victim to its own cleverness. It has concluded that a person is no more than a computer linked to an animal. And that this strange and wonderful being has no meaning beyond the present.

In this setting, the traditional belief of Christians in life beyond death seems almost quaint – or a piece of baseless optimism, whistling in the dark. Yet it persists. It still has power to bring comfort and reassurance, and the hope of it still shapes noble and sacrificial lives. I suspect that many modern people would *like* to believe it is true, but feel that modern knowledge has demolished it. A survey of religious belief in Britain carried out for BBC Radio in 1995 showed that about two-thirds of those questioned believed in life after death – interestingly, the number believing in it showed a slight decline in older age-groups.

Generally surveys of public opinion in the West over the last three decades have tended to show a diminishing number of people who express a belief in life after death. Even religious people, church-goers of all denominations, express doubts about it. On the whole, churches avoid the subject, except at funerals – and even then it is often carefully ignored. In trying to attract people to the Christian faith, the prospect of heaven is held up as an incentive to belief almost as seldom as the prospect of hell. Christians are very sensitive about the old communist jibe about offering 'pie in the sky when you die', so on the whole they avoid the subject altogether.

It's the argument of this book – based on the themes of the original *Hereafter* – that there is no logical or rational reason for this reticence. Nothing in modern scientific discovery, nothing of what we now know about human nature, the mind or the body, rules out the possibility of life beyond death in the way that the Christian faith understands it. Indeed, when the belief is properly understood and appreciated, it makes sense of much that, without it, is nonsense, and provides the meaning and purpose for life, without which it is, in Russell's words, 'triviality for a moment, and then nothing'.

Most of those who now reject the idea of 'survival' after death have been consciously or subconsciously influenced by materialistic science. This is the approach which has been characterised as 'nothing-buttery' – as in, 'existence is matter, and *nothing but* matter'. Or, 'human beings are clever animals, and *nothing but* animals'. With this approach, it becomes easy to ridicule any talk of 'soul' or 'self' as arguing for the 'ghost in the human machine' that Gilbert Ryle dismissed so categorically. I am a body, and *nothing but* a body.

Of course, many of the old ideas about the soul and immortality – about 'heavenly mansions above the bright blue sky' – are wrong, at the factual, scientific level. 'Above the bright blue sky' is a lot more sky, and then a lot more: millions of light years of it, in fact. But into rejecting superstitious, crude and pseudo-religious notions such as these, many people have also rejected the whole concept of a life beyond this life, entered into through what we call death. And in rejecting that, they have lost a priceless element of truth, which offers dignity and meaning to human life.

I hope that this book may help to bring it back: to show that, properly understood, there is nothing intrinsically impossible, or even unlikely, about 'life after death'. Indeed, that many modern insights and discoveries make it easier to accept now than it could ever have been for people a century ago. In fact, I would argue that to reject out of hand the very idea of life after death is unreasonable prejudice, demanding just the kind of closed mind which agnostics dislike so much in some religious believers.

Life beyond death is, I believe, an essential part of the Christian good news. Indeed, according to the great apostle St Paul, without it faith is futile and human life 'pitiable'. And it is a part of the Christian faith that modern people need as much as, or more than, those of earlier generations. It is a belief that transforms not just our attitude to death, but also to the whole of life. It all looks different to the person who believes that it's going somewhere.

So this book is a simple, short and provocative attempt to encourage modern people to look again at something that has meant so much to past generations, but has been thrown away as a pretty but useless toy by this one. Not for the first time in human history, we may well find that the thing we have thrown away is the thing we needed most.

1

THINKING ABOUT DEATH

I was visiting her in hospital. A devout Christian, she had suffered many years of illness and now felt convinced that the end was near.

'I've been thinking a lot,' she said, 'here in bed. About . . . well, what may lie ahead. I mean, we don't *know*, do we? The resurrection of the body, life after death, heaven and all that. It's all right when you're singing about it in church, but when you come to . . . this point . . . it looks a bit different.'

As we talked, I recognised that she, perhaps on the doorstep of the next life, and myself, who to be honest seldom gave it more than a passing thought, actually shared the same fears. We both 'believed' in eternal life, because as Christians it was part of the 'package'. But when it came to the crunch, looking through the doorway into an invisible and unknown future, we were only aware of apprehension and misgivings.

Was that a denial of faith? That was what we talked about, and slowly came to recognise that there was all the difference in the world between believing that something was so – and even that it was on balance

1

a good thing – and actually *wanting it to happen*. And the difference was the difference between the known and the unknown.

That is the real terror associated with dying. It is completely outside our experience. It is always and inevitably something that happens to other people, not to us. So however much we may believe and even in a sense joyfully anticipate a future filled with the love and presence of God, at the moment when it becomes imminent we are bound to be apprehensive.

I have friends who have just emigrated to New Zealand, to join their married daughter. They have longed and worked for the day when it would happen, made their plans, been impatient for the date to be fixed. Yet on the eve of their departure you could see the anxiety. Will it be as we anticipate? Will we settle in? What about all the friends we're leaving behind – not to speak of the house, the village and the familiar sights and sounds of Britain? New Zealand is hardly 'the unknown', but still the moment of transition could create apprehension.

I'm told it's the same with the baby in the womb. For nine months it has had a blissfully secure regime, fed as need arose, sheltered in a cosy and warm environment, soothed by the rhythmic beating of its mother's heart. In one way life in the womb is perfect.

Yet the moment comes when the baby must be thrust out of the womb. In a few hours of traumatic struggle it leaves its warmth and security and finds itself in a strange world of lights and noise. Suddenly all is strange and terrifying. Mother's heartbeat is no longer all around. No wonder the baby's first response to birth is to bawl its head off!

Some experts have suggested that the baby in the womb is in fact reluctant to be born – and that the experience of birth is a trauma which affects our subconscious all through life. And yet, looking back, who would really prefer life enclosed in a protective bag to the experience of life in the open air? The possibilities in the womb are extremely limited. The possibilities of life in the world are almost infinite. The baby in the womb will never see a sunset, crack a joke with friends, dance or play or make love. Yet, because it is unknown, that life which seems so 'normal' to us may well seem strange and terrifying to the baby.

Could it be that death is more like birth than we imagine? Is it possible that our fear of it is very like the anxiety of the unborn baby faced with an unknown future?

The baby really does know nothing at all about life in the outside world. And many modern people would say exactly the same about the 'life to come' – it's utterly obscure, totally beyond our experience or knowledge. Yet past generations, who knew nothing at all about magnetism or radio waves or atomic particles, seemed to have satisfying and convincing answers to the question of their ultimate destiny.

It seems a long way from the days when the ambition of many a Christian person was to 'make a good death'. His modern counterpart spends his life trying to postpone it and hoping that when it comes it will be sudden and unexpected. We speak with envy of those who die instantly of a heart attack: she 'knew nothing about it', it was 'mercifully swift'. We conspire to keep from the dying person a knowledge of their true condition and when the end comes we try to see that it disturbs or upsets as few people as possible. Death is not a friend, but an implacable enemy, to be fought off with all the considerable weaponry of modern skill and knowledge.

Yet thinking about death is not really a negative, morbid thing to do. In one sense, it is the necessary key to contentment, because if we cannot face our end, the whole journey towards it is corrupted by anxiety. It's not really possible to live a completely happy life without considering its destination.

If you decide, as many people in history have, that it's actually going nowhere, it's possible to live with a brave acceptance that the present is all that there is. But if you come to the conclusion that this life has meaning and purpose, and that its ultimate destiny is with the God who created it, then the whole of existence is transformed. It seems more positive, and for me more in line with the evidence, to take that position.

After all, human life, in terms of cosmic time, is a mere spitting of a tiny spark in the darkness, so brief that it can hardly be seen. Yet those brief human lives have achieved so much: beauty, art, creativity, holiness. It is hard to accept that the destiny of those human lives – so short, and yet so significant – is to turn to dust on the surface of this tiny planet. That would suggest that creation has achieved its highest goal and then thrown it away like a child throwing away a broken doll.

So the question 'Why?' is still the most important one we can ask. Why do we exist? Does human life have a meaning? Have we been created for a greater destiny than eighty or ninety years of bodily existence? Is death the end, or a beginning?

Those are the questions I want to address in the next chapters. At the end, you may agree with me, or may decide that the case is· unproven. But at least you will have given it serious thought. What is really unworthy is to go right through our life on earth and never seriously ask ourselves whether our journey meant nothing, anything . . . or everything.

2

'WHAT HAPPENS WHEN I DIE?'

There are any number of books to tell me what will happen when I get married, have a baby, or reach retirement age. But there are very few to tell me what will happen when I die. At one level, that's understandable. After all, there are any number of married people, parents and pensioners around to give us the benefit of their experience. But we aren't similarly surrounded by people who have experienced death.

Yet dying is more common than marriage, parenthood or retirement. Not everybody experiences those, but *everybody*, without exception, experiences death. Along with birth, it's the most common human experience.

Or perhaps we would say that death is not part of human experience – that what happens when I die is that I cease to 'happen' any more, so there isn't much to say about it. The famous philosopher Wittgenstein put it like this: 'In death, the world does not change, but ceases. *Death is not an event in life.*'

So why have a book to tell me that at a certain date in the future, at present unknown to me, I shall cease to exist? Indeed, if that were the case, it would be a pointless and rather depressing volume – hardly a bestseller.

But for the Christian, and for people of most other religions, too, death is most emphatically *not* the end. Far from not being 'an event in life' it is almost *the* event, the moment of progress onward and into a new kind of existence. Far from being the end of the world, it is the beginning of a new one.

The great psychologist, Jung, said that a belief in immortality had therapeutic power, because 'no-one can live in peace in a house that he knows is shortly to tumble about his ears'. So he saw belief in life beyond death as a healthy, positive and 'therapeutic' thing, enabling people to live and die with dignity, and to think about death not as the arch-enemy but as a gateway to a fuller life. That doesn't make it true, of course, but it does suggest that to ignore the subject altogether and simply concentrate on postponing the inevitable as long as we can is an unhealthy, negative and even destructive approach to death.

'Unless the certainty of death is taken clearly into consciousness and faced squarely,' wrote Erastus Evans, 'it is impossible for the old person to live the last years of life with peace and dignity.' That suggests that our attempts to ignore death are psychologically damaging, but that coming to terms with its reality, and especially seeing it as a positive experience, is the way to confidence and peace of mind.

However, the fact that belief in life after death helps

us to adjust emotionally to the idea of death is no argument for or against the truth of it. I suspect there may sometimes be a hint of a conspiracy, perhaps involving Christian ministers, relatives and friends of an elderly or dying person, to 'talk up' the idea of life after death. Of course it is comforting to be told that 'heaven' is just around the corner and that death is a doorway into a fuller life. But it's an empty comfort if there's no truth in it – and the tactic of talking as though it's true but secretly doubting whether it is suffers the consequences of the law of diminishing returns. Each time we use it, it becomes less convincing. And when those who have used it to offer empty comfort to the dying come to that moment themselves, it has no power to help.

What I am saying is that the crucial question is not 'Does belief in life after death help us to face death?' – it obviously does – but, 'Is it true?' For modern people, shaped by the culture of our times, there is no other option. We can't call on a tribal tradition or an accepted folk-story which has lain there dormant in our subconscious since childhood 'until required'. They simply do not exist.

We have to face the more difficult, but ultimately more rewarding question, 'What is the truth of the matter?' Facing that honestly may well be the preparation we need for facing death honestly. If we decide there is no life beyond, then we can grit our metaphorical teeth and greet the inevitable with dignity and courage. If we decide that there *is* life beyond the grave, then the whole business of death and dying assumes a different perspective. There is hope – not an illusion built on self-deception or the kind conspiracy of well-meaning friends, but solid and reliable hope.

Facing death requires some understanding of what death is. Strangely, it's quite hard to define, yet everyone knows what the word means – even quite small children. Death, in ordinary language, simply means the end of life. Flowers, pets and birds die, and we see the result of death in shrivelled plants and lifeless and decaying bodies.

Death occurs in a human being when a spontaneous heartbeat can't be restored and when brain activity has ceased, with no possibility of regained consciousness. Modern medicine has made what was once clear-cut into something of a grey zone, because it is now possible to keep people 'alive' according to both of these definitions when they are, for all practical purposes, dead. But these are borderline cases, painful and distressing for relatives and doctors, but still mercifully rare. For the most part, not only doctors but lay people too know when a person, or an animal, is 'dead'.

Death, as we have just defined it, happens to the body. It is the body that dies. Weary and literally worn out, or brought low by disease, or struck down by accident or violence, it 'gives up the ghost', and very soon it has all but disappeared. The moment death comes, disintegration begins. It's as though nature can't wait to complete its cycle and recover the chemical riches which for a life-time have been stored in the body.

So what happens to the body at death is quite simply that it changes from being a living thing to a dead one, and its physical disintegration begins. Of course, in one sense it has already begun, because all our adult lives we are 'dying', as the process of growing old goes on. But death is its crisis. We all know that, and it's as well to face it – bluntly, if need be. Whatever hope the Christian faith holds out for the future of personality (or the 'self'), it holds out none at all for the body in which that personality or 'self' has expressed itself on earth. In the memorable words of Ecclesiastes, 'then the dust returns to the earth as it was.'[1] We go back to what we were at the beginning: 'dust to dust'.

I realise that some people will be rather shocked by that statement. Doesn't the Christian faith speak of the resurrection of the body? And didn't Handel in the *Messiah* put marvellous music to words from the Bible that assert that 'though worms destroy this body, yet in my flesh will I see God'[2]?

Yes, the Christian faith does speak of the resurrection of the body, but not the resuscitation of corpses. To that we shall return in some detail later. And yes, Handel did set music to words from the King James Version of the Bible, which translate a notoriously obscure piece of Hebrew text from the book of Job. Most modern translations read something like: 'After my skin has been destroyed, then *without my flesh* [or,

11

from my flesh] I shall see God.' Nobody can be absolutely sure what the original author meant to convey, but I think we can be certain that the reconstruction of Job's skin, flesh and bones after death was not what he had in mind. It would have been an idea completely foreign to the Jewish understanding of what happened after death at that stage of its development.

Certainly the teaching of the New Testament on life after death sees our future as real people, not wispy ghosts, but that future is not going to be limited by these earth-bound time capsules which we call our bodies. Every time we say the words 'Ashes to ashes, dust to dust' at a grave-side we are recognising that the human body is mortal and its destiny is inevitably linked to the earth.

So at death the body dies. It is discarded – with due respect, one hopes – and very soon disintegrates. The 'dust returns to the earth as it was'. But that leaves the second half of that intriguing verse from the generally rather pessimistic book of Ecclesiastes: 'And the spirit returns to God, who gave it.' Whatever the author meant, it is in line with the whole thrust of the Bible's teaching to claim that here is the real distinction between the 'nothing-butters' and the believers. Is a human being a body and *nothing but* a body? Or does something survive death, something we might call the 'spirit' of a man or woman? As the body of John Smith disintegrates, does 'anything' of John Smith remain? And if so, what?

3

SELF, SPIRIT, SOUL

The idea that a human being is a body housing a soul is at least as old as Plato. He believed that the soul existed before the body and survived the death of the body. In other words, the soul was immortal. Another Greek philosopher, Aristotle, also spoke of the soul, but thought of it as the sum total of living as a personal being. Human beings, for him, were 'psychosomatic unities' – as we might say more simply, 'whole people . . . body, mind and spirit'.

For a long while Christian theology got hung up on the Platonic idea. The soul was a gift of God to the human person. There was some argument about when it was received – at conception, at quickening, at birth – but little doubt that it existed, a kind of 'ghost' in the human machine. And, of course, the soul survived death. There were even artistic representations of the soul leaving the body, to fly up to heaven, or down to hell.

The idea persists, of course. And there is enough truth in it to ensure that it will survive. But it is not the teaching of the Bible, which does not say that humans *have* souls but that they *are* souls, which is a very different thing. As Aristotle argued, we are whole people: body, mind and spirit. So for the Bible full humanity involves all of those elements, which is why belief in the resurrection of the *body* is so central to a Christian understanding of life beyond death. But to say that human existence is incomplete without a body is not at all to say that it is *impossible*.

Back in the thirteenth century, the great theologian Aquinas, while believing that human souls exist after death, argued that they did so in a very imperfect way. Only when we got our bodies back at the final resurrection of the dead would we be 'proper persons' again. He could see the problem of disembodied souls being regarded as 'people'. Only when we have bodies can we properly be described as human beings, because only in a *body* can my 'self' express itself fully.

But that does not mean that the idea of the soul is useless, however much some modern thinkers may ridicule it. Of course you can't weigh the body before and after death and measure the substance of the soul. Of course it's foolish to think of a bank of souls from which the Creator takes one and pops it into each new human being. And of course it gives rise to all kinds of weird and wonderful ideas if we start thinking of our departed friends and relatives as existing only in the form of disembodied souls.

But people are more than simply their bodies. That is the fundamental thing to hold on to. To say that we do not 'have' souls is simply to say that we don't possess them in the way that we possess hands, feet and ears. It's not to devalue the idea of the soul, but to rescue it from superstition.

Perhaps we could put it like this. What distinguishes human beings from other living creatures is the power of understanding. We don't simply exist; we *know* that we exist. When that first occurred in the creation, something utterly new and distinctive had appeared. Arthur Peacocke, in *God and the New Biology*, even sees this development as a clue to the meaning of the universe: 'The scientific fact that matter . . . can in man become self-conscious and personal, self-transcendent and corporately self-reflective is a fundamental feature of the cosmos and must be regarded as a clue to its meaning and intelligibility.'

Clearly the Creator had rational understanding (unless the universe is the product of blind chance). God 'knows that he exists'. But now another being also knew that it existed, and we can date the emergence of what we call the 'soul' to the moment when that happened, whenever that was in the story of *Homo sapiens*.

Its existence is of fundamental importance. It marks out human persons from all the other creatures. The rational soul has the power of understanding its own existence. As Professor Keith Ward wrote in his book *The Battle for the Soul*, 'whatever possesses it is importantly different in kind from other things which do not possess it'.

So the 'soul' is really awareness of self. God has it,

of course, but *so do we*. Self-consciousness – that is, being aware that I exist – is known by introspection. I look into myself and recognise conscious being, become aware that I am *me*. That consciousness is what makes me human, but it is also what unites me to God, because it mirrors his own self-consciousness. God exists. He is aware that he exists. That's more or less what his name in Hebrew – *Yahweh* – means: the 'existing One'. 'I am who I am'[1] is how one Bible translates it. And that is why we regard God as a Person, not a 'thing' or a 'force'. Among all his creatures there is one – and to the best of our present knowledge, only one – that shares that self-consciousness. We, too, are *persons*. Surely that is why, in the story of creation in the Bible, only men and women – of all the created beings – are described as 'made in the image of God'.[2]

That consciousness doesn't simply relate to the present. Human beings differ from things and from animals in that we are aware of the past as well as the present, and we anticipate the future. Of course, squirrels store nuts for the winter and birds build nests for their, as yet, unborn young. But they have no sense (so far as we know) of any long-term destiny. They are fulfilling an instinctive drive. Only beings who know who they are, and where they are from, can have any sense of where they are going.

So a human being has two unbreakable 'links'. We are linked to the animal creation, through our bodies – which include our brains. And we are linked to the Creator himself through our 'souls'. With the animals we share many physical attributes – bodies, brains, instincts, systems. With God we share the most important thing of all: we know that we exist, we have the power of understanding, we are known to ourselves, we are conscious of our own being.

Bodies, as we have seen, die. We know what becomes of them – they cease to exist. But if consciousness is an attribute of God himself, then it can't cease to exist. It is through the will of the Creator that we are able to know ourselves. He has made us *persons*. And nothing can destroy that knowledge. If we think of the soul as 'self', as the awareness or consciousness of existing, and if we accept that that is an attribute of God himself, then 'soul' or 'self' can no more cease to exist than God himself can cease to exist.

A 'simpler' argument

This has been quite an obscure argument! So let me try to put it in a simpler, more down-to-earth way. We are all familiar with the idea of the 'soul' – 'God rest her soul', and so on. When we say that, we're assuming that there is something of 'her' which is distinct from her body, something we call 'soul'. And that that, at least, can survive death. We probably think of it as a pretty creepy idea – Dracula, and that kind of thing! And most of us probably would not fancy the idea of an existence after death that 'reduced' us to being no more than disembodied 'soul'. That would seem to

17

consign us to the shadowy world of ghosts, drifting about on the edge of reality. Our future would be in the world of dreams, not the world of real existence.

So it's quite a relief to discover that that is not at all what the Bible promises. It does not separate off 'soul' from the body. It doesn't see us as 'souls' living like tenants in bodies, but as whole people. Yet within that 'whole person' there is an element which we can properly distinguish as 'soul' – that element of my existence that makes me *me* . . . my 'self', as we might say.

And that is what, in the biblical view of things, survives death. Not a 'soul', in the sense of some wispy spirit being, but *me*, the person I am – myself. And if you break that word 'myself' into its two parts you will see what I am getting at: my *self*. The clue to the whole thing is that word 'self'. When I speak of 'myself' I'm recognising that I exist. And if that sounds obvious, it's actually one of the most important truths about our existence. *We know that we exist*.

Why is that so important? Because until God created human beings no-one and nothing in the universe knew that it existed *except God himself*. When he made people 'in his own image' he gave them the same unique ability that he had, not just to exist (animals and plants exist, and are alive) but to *know that they exist*.

God can't die. He can't cease to exist, because he is him-*self*. But he has created you and me as 'selves', too: your-*self*, my-*self*. And that can't cease to exist, either.

18

But how can it continue to exist without a body? How can 'self' mean anything at all without a body in which to express itself? Aren't we back at the idea of disembodied souls? Can we in any way visualise being conscious selves *without* a body?

Keith Ward, in *The Battle for the Soul*, deals with this very objection. 'Although it (the soul, or self) needs some form of embodiment to have things to think about, it is separate from any particular body, and it could exist in an imperfect way without it. Perhaps the best example is in dreaming, when I at least imagine myself continuing to exist, though not in this particular body.' He might have added that the dreamer sometimes 'sees' themselves in a dream, perhaps lying asleep in the bed!

As Keith Ward says, dreaming is an 'imperfect' way of existing. Few of us would like to think that our destiny beyond the grave was a kind of dream-like existence. But at least the experience of dreaming does show that we can 'function' apart from our bodies, even if in a limited way. Fortunately, as we have already mentioned, the Bible doesn't hold out the prospect of a bodiless future! Resurrection, as we shall see later, is the Christian view of life beyond death, and that requires the reuniting of our soul/self with a body, so that we can fully express ourselves and 'exist' in a truly human and complete way.

Human existence is very wonderful, but most of us take it for granted. We share with animals our anatomy, senses, appetites, instincts, physiology, methods of reproduction and so on, and we share with machines many other attributes. Our limbs are perfect examples of engineering, our eyes are the finest cameras yet invented, our brains are superb and highly compact computers. But we are more than an animal and more than a machine. And the 'plus', the thing that not only distinguishes a human being from a machine or an animal but even from another human being, is *personality*.

What makes Janet Brown different from Sandra Jones is not some complicated theory about person-hood, but a menu of qualities and attributes that we recognise as 'hers' (and notice the possessive pronoun – they are 'hers', and nobody else's). This goes far beyond physical appearance, which over the years can change drastically. It includes her beliefs, characteristics, preferences, skills, interests and emotions. It involves love and affection, feelings, attitudes and choices. So the 'real' Janet Brown, who loves her husband and children and enjoys sunsets and growing roses, is distinct from the 'real' Sandra Jones, who has many special friends but no 'partner', and who prefers music to sunsets and driving her sports car to growing roses. They are both distinctive people. They are *persons*, and that is another way of saying that they are self-conscious beings, in the way that God is. And it is that person that survives death, not as a fleeting spirit, but as – well, Janet Brown and Sandra Jones.

In his book *The Search for God* the distinguished scientist Sir John Houghton offers another, and perhaps more up-to-date, way of visualising this distinction between self and body. He compares the human situation to a computer, where you have 'hardware' (the silicon chips, wires, discs and tape stores, keyboards and so on) and 'software' (the programs which manipulate, and even learn from, the input data and organise the output of the data store). Software is no use by itself. It must have hardware through which to 'express itself'.

As he pointed out – and many of us have learnt to our cost! – hardware has a limited life. It wears out. Software, on the other hand, can be transferred to new hardware – perhaps better, more advanced hardware, where it can have more scope and its capabilities can be extended.

He suggests that the body is like computer hardware, providing both input and output devices, through our senses, limbs and speech, and also a processor and storage vehicle in our brains. Our 'self' is the software, some of it built in from the start (through our genes), some of it generated during our lives through interaction with other people, our individual choices, and so on. When we die our bodies, the 'hardware', wear out, but through the process of resurrection our self, the 'software', is transferred to a new means of expression, what Christians call the 'resurrection body'. And there, like software in a more sophisticated piece of hardware, the self will have more scope and fulfil all its capabilities.

Is this kind of belief rational? The late Professor

Donald Mackay was one of Britain's foremost experts in the communications systems of the human brain. As a Christian, he believed in life beyond death, and this is how he saw it:

It is not as disembodied spirits that God promises us eternal life, but as personalities expressed in a new kind of body – what the apostle Paul calls a 'spiritual body'. Just as a message is still the same message whether it's spoken in words or flashed in morse code, so, according to the Bible, we shall be the same persons, whatever the material form in which our personalities may be expressed. Nothing in the scientific picture of man, however complete it may one day become, could affect the truth of this doctrine one way or the other.

So Professor Mackay saw personality as a kind of 'message', and our present bodies as one means of 'transmitting' that message. But like all Christians he looks on to a new kind of body, a better 'transmitter' – more advanced 'hardware' – in a new kind of life beyond death.

And this is precisely what the Bible itself teaches. The survival of personality – of self or soul – is what Christianity asserts, and that this personality expresses itself in the 'life beyond' in a new form suited to its new environment. As a belief, this one fits the available facts and answers the ultimate questions at least as well as, and probably a great deal better than, any other theory about life and death that the human race has yet devised.

Of course, this belief could be seen as terribly egocentric. I am so important that I must go on living for ever! And sometimes Christians can catch themselves thinking and talking like that. But the clue to it all is our dependence on God. Our continued existence depends upon his continued existence, not on our cleverness or goodness. This means, of course, that the fulfilment of individual existence is not going to be self-indulgence, but what we might call 'living like God'. And as his life expresses itself most completely in love that loses itself by pouring itself out, we may assume that our lives with him in eternity will be based on the same principle. There's not much room for self-indulgence or egocentricity there!

That is the Christian position, as clearly as I can set it out, and I believe that it is the teaching of the Bible. In following chapters I shall try to justify that claim and then, in rather more detail, attempt to answer the question, 'In what kind of a body will we live out our existence beyond death?' But first I would like to consider the whole question of the survival of human personality after death. It there really any sound *evidence* for it?

4

EVIDENCE FOR SURVIVAL

The evidence against survival after death is simple and strong. It's the evidence of our own eyes. When a bird, or a goldfish, or a plant, or a person dies, life has ended. Death is the 'end', and if it isn't, then it isn't death. As we've seen, the medical world may argue about the precise definition of death, but a ten-year-old knows exactly what it is. You may preserve the form of something that has died, but its life is gone.

In the nature of things, the evidence for survival is not so simply expressed. It has to overcome the apparently overwhelming evidence of our senses. And, of course, it asks us to accept the elusive distinction between 'body' and 'self' or 'soul', which was the subject of the last chapter.

Yet in fact the evidence is very strong. I remember reading with astonishment an article in *The Humanist* nearly thirty years ago, in which a Dr John Beloff argued very persuasively that Humanists should accept that 'survival' after death occurs, but find a non-religious explanation for it. If they didn't, he warned, the evidence for survival might 'one day present a challenge to Humanism as profound in its own way as that which Darwinian Evolution did to Christianity a century ago'.

What is that evidence, and why did an atheist find it so convincing? The last thirty years have seen it grow, as modern medicine has increased the number of people who have experienced 'near-death' phenomena and research has increased into the paranormal. If Dr Beloff were writing now, he might feel that his prediction was beginning to be fulfilled.

The Society for Psychical Research, whose brief is to investigate in a scientific and controlled way any kind of psychic manifestation, has amassed an enormous amount of carefully documented evidence on the subject. Contrary to what one might think, its members are not by any means all 'spiritualists', or even religious believers. Some are agnostic about survival, but wish to see the evidence about it properly and rationally examined.

Now of course a great deal of the kind of 'evidence' which the Society for Physical Research has accumulated amounts to little more than personal anecdote – people who claim to have seen ghosts, and so on. It's easy to be sceptical about such evidence, but if there is enough of it, and it offers some kind of a consistent pattern, then it should not be entirely discounted. And much of the evidence is not so easily dismissed.

A good deal of it does, of course, relate to what is usually called 'spiritualism'. Orthodox Christians tend – rightly, in my judgment – to steer clear of 'spiritualist' activities, which are specifically and sternly forbidden in the Bible.[1] But the fact remains that, among a great deal that is obviously either fraudulent or a matter of self-deception, there is a body of well-documented phenomena which suggests that human personality is not always extinguished at death.

I remember interviewing, for a radio programme on Spiritualism, a number of people who had attended seances. Making due allowance for self-deception – it is desperately easy to hear what you *want* to hear – and for the skill of the medium in presenting vague generalisations as though they were a private message, I had to admit that from time to time it was impossible to imagine any source of the information they had received other than the dead person. As I have said, I don't think that the ability of mediums sometimes to contact the spirits of dead people is a valid reason for consulting them, but I think it is irrational to ignore such evidence as Spiritualism offers about 'survival'.

However, the evidence for survival goes far beyond the world of seances and mediums. In a book published in 1961, *The Evidence of Psychical Research Concerning Survival*, W. H. Slater relates one of the most convincing and best-documented accounts of communication from the other side of death. It is known as the Chaffin Will Case.

James Chaffin, a farmer in North Carolina, died in 1921 as the result of a fall, leaving a widow and two sons. In 1905 he made a will leaving his

whole property to his third son, Marshall, who
proved the will and himself died about a year
later, leaving a widow and a son, a minor. In June
1925 the second son, James, began to have vivid
dreams of his father appearing at his bedside and
speaking. This vision may have been a 'border-
land' experience, occurring between sleeping and
waking. It was more realistic than pure dreams
usually are but in an experience as informative
as this the distinction is of little importance.

The figure was dressed in a black overcoat
which James had often seen his father wearing.
[James said that] 'He often took hold of his
overcoat this way and pulled it back and said,
"You will find my will in my overcoat pocket"
and then disappeared.'

James went to his elder brother's house and
found the coat, and inside the inner pocket,
which was sewn up, a roll of paper with the
words, 'Read the 27th chapter of Genesis in my
daddie's old Bible.' James found the old Bible in a
drawer in his mother's house and in the presence
of witnesses found between two folded pages on
which the 27th chapter of Genesis was printed
another will, dated January 16th 1919, whereby
the Testator, 'after reading the 27th chapter of
Genesis, in which the supplanting of Esau by
Jacob is related,' divided his property equally
between his four sons and added, 'You must
take care of your Mammy'.

The second will, though unattested by witnesses, was valid by the law of the State ...
Before probate, however, the Testator appeared
again to his son James, saying 'Where is my old
will?' and showing 'considerable temper'.

This account is, I realise, an old one, but I have used
it because, unlike many of those pieces of anecdotal
evidence to which I referred earlier, it is very well
documented. However sceptical the reader, it is hard
to think of an explanation that doesn't include some
communication – of whatever kind – between a dead
person and a living one. Old James Chaffin was
unarguably dead, and had been so for four years,
when he managed to communicate to young James
the location of his will. It would seem to follow that,
in the normal sense of the word, he wasn't 'dead' at
all, even though his body most certainly was. At any
rate, something of old James Chaffin had survived
death and was able to communicate an intelligible
and coherent message.

'Near-death' experiences

Recently there has been a great deal of interest in what
are called 'near-death' experiences. With the advance
of resuscitation techniques, many patients who, by old
definitions, would be considered to have 'died' are in
fact 'brought back to life'. Extensive surveys, based on

literally hundreds of cases, have shown a remarkable consistency in the way people have subsequently described their experiences while 'dead'.

While a few have reported frightening images, which some of them associated with punishment or hell, the vast majority – whether they were formally religious or not – told of an experience of great joy and peace, with a heightened awareness both of themselves and of their surroundings. They were drawn towards a bright light, which often revealed itself as the figure of a person of enormous love and goodness, who welcomed them. Many of the respondents identified this 'person' as Jesus. When the medical treatment their body was receiving began to take effect, they were disappointed to find themselves being drawn away from this place of light and beauty back into the 'ordinary' world.

There are many published accounts along these lines (some of which are listed in the bibliography at the end of this book). And there have been many attempts to 'explain' them, both by religious people keen to find their own beliefs confirmed and by sceptics offering various medical or psychological explanations of these experiences. So it is probably dangerous to claim too much for what are, at best, subjective reports. But it is also foolish, and prejudiced, to ignore a large body of evidence, often describing almost identical experiences, simply because it doesn't fit in with our preconceptions about what can and cannot happen.

There have been a number of attempts to examine and analyse such experiences on a scientific basis. In the late 1970s two Americans, Otis and Haraldson, conducted a massive and controlled survey of what they called 'visions' or 'hallucinations' on the part of terminally ill or near-death patients. Initially this involved doctors – over 1,700 responded – and then wherever possible interviews with patients. The results were published in a book (*At the Hour of Death*, 1977) and were the subject of a follow-up article in the British *Nursing Mirror*, a professional journal for nurses.

The conclusions reached by Otis and Haraldson as a result of this survey may help us to evaluate the 'evidence' offered by such near-death experiences. 'The visions described', they wrote, 'seem to suggest that the dying person has a glimpse of the after-life or heaven, which is not apparent to others around. It is clear though that the apparitions vary according to the beliefs of the individual.' The authors rejected notions that the visions were wish-fulfilments, in that the apparitions (of people who had already died) were 'more often than not of someone the patient did not particularly want to see'. They summarise the position in these words: 'It would seem that the visions remain a mystery. Scientifically, it would be difficult to demonstrate that the visions were of actual entities. They seem to be hallucinations and are only observed by the patient, yet they are not readily explicable by physiological or psychological causes.'

Among these 'near death' reports there are few where any external tests can be applied. As we have seen, they are mostly entirely subjective: people's accounts of their own memories of a particularly vivid kind. But that is not true of all of them, and I have had personal contact with a man who had, over forty years ago, a near-death experience where a number of the claims he made were verified at the time by medical witnesses. I think his story is worth relating in some detail. I first met him in 1976, when we broadcast it on BBC Radio, and everything about it, and him, convinced me of its authenticity.

Edmund Wilbourne was, at the time when this happened, a very young Church Army officer in Lancashire. He was critically ill in Crumpsall Hospital with pleurisy and pneumonia. He died, and was in fact certified dead and his body 'laid out' by one of the nurses on the ward. At that point, he reports, he seemed to leave his body and could actually observe the nurse preparing his body for the mortuary. Later he was able to identify correctly not only which nurse it was but also precisely what she did.

He felt linked to the body on the bed by a cord, but then the cord was severed and he arrived at a 'place' which he took to be heaven. It was, in his own words, 'nothing like floating on clouds or harps or anything of that sort', but a place of activity and meaning. 'I felt more alive and more alert than I've ever done since', he said.

Then he saw Jesus, recognising him by the print of the nails in his hands and feet – as he thought at the time, they were 'the only man-made things in heaven'. He recognised other people, too, friends who had died, and was not at all pleased when an insistent voice grew louder and louder, praying 'O God, don't let him die, he's got work to do for you.' Finally, as he explained, 'the Lord Jesus turned me round on my shoulder and gave me a gentle push, saying something to the effect that "it's not time for you yet".' Edmund Wilbourne came round in the hospital mortuary, two hours after he had been certified dead.

Subsequently he described his experience of what he took to be heaven. It was a place of intense light and activity, with Jesus 'light itself', and yet very definitely a 'person', in the same way as the other people he recognised: his Sunday School teacher, his mother and grandmother, and his doctor, who had died just previously. While they had what he called 'physical shape', it somehow combined the youth and vigour of a young person with a sense of perfect maturity.

It's immediately obvious that Captain Wilbourne's account is very similar to many others. Like them he describes an 'out-of-the-body' experience, which is very vivid and clear. There is the place of intense light and the welcoming figure. And, of course, there is the marked reluctance to return to the 'ordinary' world. The 'voice' he heard praying while he was in 'heaven' turned out to have been that of his landlady, who at that moment was kneeling by her bed praying that God would 'spare' him for the work she believed Edmund had yet to do for God.

But while his account is similar to many others, it is still one of the most compelling. For one thing, it

33

occurred, and was medically documented, long before the more recent interest in the subject of near-death experiences. He had no 'models' to copy. For another, he was extremely reluctant to talk about it. He waited well over twenty years before telling his story publicly. And, of course, there was the corroborating evidence of the nurses and medical staff at Crumpsall Hospital.

Having met him and discussed this experience with him, I have no doubt about the genuineness of his experience. He is a calm, sober and self-effacing person who has not added anything to this account over the years. The story has remained the same, as vivid forty years after the event as it was when it first happened.

His account, and the many others like it, are not 'scientific' evidence, of course. However, when many sane and balanced people, over a long period of time but in roughly similar circumstances, record very much the same experience, one must attach some weight to it. Certainly the almost universal testimony to the experience of the body and 'self' becoming separated is highly relevant to any discussion of the question of the survival of the 'self' after death.

So much of the evidence about survival falls into this kind of category. Each piece taken on its own can be refuted, but taken together they all seem to point one way. And that is not surprising, really. After all, against all the evidence of our eyes, the vast majority of human beings throughout history have believed that there was life beyond death, whether it's the *Valhalla* of the Norsemen or the Elysian Fields of the Romans. The funeral rites of our remote cave-dwelling ancestors suggest that they were preparing the dead for some future life, and that kind of preparation can be found in the tombs of the ancient Egyptians and the burial mounds of the ancient Britons.

As a race, we have clung to this apparently irrational belief. Even in our modern scientific world, the great majority of people believe in some kind of life beyond death. It is hard to account for this unless it responds to some deep, inner longing – a reluctance, I suppose, to accept that human life is so unimportant that it can peter out in a handful of dust after sixty, seventy, eighty or whatever years.

Of course, the presence of such a universal longing doesn't prove that it corresponds to the facts. Yet, as the late Leslie Weatherhead once pointed out, 'In a rational universe a universal longing seems to me to be a kind of signpost pointing in the direction of the satisfaction of the wish.' He continued, 'If the world is a rational place, that fact that I feel hungry seems to me to point to the fact that there is such a thing as food. The terrific hunger for sex seems, in a rational world, to point to the fact that there is such a thing as the happiness of sexual fulfilment. Similarly the desire to go on after death at any rate points in the direction that it is likely.'

There are also what we might call philosophical arguments for the idea that 'soul' or 'self' is not the same thing as 'brain' or 'body', and can therefore survive beyond death. Most of these arguments were set out in an important book, *The Elusive Mind*, written by H. D. Lewis in 1969. If the mind and brain are identical – that's to say, if the brain dies so does the mind of the person – there is no way to check the theory, because the mind would be no more than a computer (simply a function of brain cells), and a computer cannot check the validity of its own programming.

Not only that, but we do in fact all act as though there were a 'self' over and above our bodies. As all the cells in my body are different now from what they were just seven years ago, if 'body' and 'self' are the same thing that would mean that I am a completely different 'self' from the one I was then. Yet I know that that isn't so. I am the same person, even though every single cell in my body has been replaced, and I accept responsibility for what I did seven years ago. It was *me*!

A third point is rather more elusive, yet it mirrors our experience perfectly. It is that we can only experience 'self' or 'soul' from *inside*. I can only begin to understand what it means by referring to my own experience of being 'myself'. No-one working from 'outside', as it were, can possibly analyse 'self'. Consequently, scientific method, which studies things from their external and material aspect, can't cope with the idea of self. Yet every single human being 'has' it, knows he or she has it, and lives life as though it were a fact. You don't have to teach a three-year-old the theory of self-hood!

Strangely enough, many ordinary people who have been bereaved can testify very vividly to the truth that lies behind these rather elusive theories. Time and again one hears them say, 'I feel he is here all the time' or 'I honestly feel she has never left me.' I have often asked people, a month or two after the funeral, whether they think the one who has died has 'ceased to exist'. In every case – I believe, without exception – they have replied very firmly, 'Certainly not.'

In an interesting book published in Belgium on the psychology of death and the afterlife, A. Godin quotes a letter from a Brussels businessman whose mother had died ten months earlier:

> Since my mother died, we find that she has become even more present to us than formerly. My wife and children also feel that the goodness we read in her eyes till the end, and the hope that her words always expressed, are now diffused in the family atmosphere which we breathe. We no longer think of her as someone who has passed away . . .

That puts very eloquently what many people try to express. I think the experience explains the popularity of those words of Henry Scott Holland which are so often read at funeral services – sometimes to the irritation of the clergy, I have to say!

I have only slipped away into the next room. I am I and you are you. Whatever we were to each other that we still are . . . Life means all that it ever meant. It is the same as it ever was; there is absolutely unbroken continuity. Why should I be out of mind because I am out of sight? I am waiting for you for an interval, somewhere very near, just around the corner. All is well.

The reason some clergy don't like it is that it may discourage people from coming to terms with the reality of bereavement. Their loved one has died, but the notion of their still being 'in the next room' may make it more difficult for them to accept that that is so. And, of course, this picture falls far short of the splendid vision of life with God which is the true Christian understanding about the destiny of the believing dead.

But it corresponds with uncanny accuracy to how many people *feel*. They *know* that the one they loved who has died has not ceased to exist, and from time to time they are conscious of them in much the same way as they were when they were alive. I realise that that is very subjective 'evidence', but again one has to say that when enough people experience it the wise enquirer does not dismiss it out of hand.

So where does this look at some of the evidence for 'survival' leave us? Of course it has not proved life beyond death: that is impossible this side of the grave. But equally it has shown that there are good and convincing reasons for believing it. We may end up agreeing with the verdict of the late Professor Sir Cyril Burt, who wrote that one important result of psychological and para-psychological investigations was to have demonstrated '*at least the possibility* of survival in some form or other, though not necessarily in the form depicted by traditional piety or fourth-century metaphysics'.

But one important, and I would say, crucial piece of evidence remains, so important that it must have a chapter all to itself. I refer to the question of the resurrection from the dead of Jesus. Because if it happened, as Christians assert, then we *do* have some evidence 'from the other side of the grave'. One 'traveller' *has* returned to tell the tale. Death is not necessarily the end. So much hangs on what we decide about the resurrection of Jesus.

5

THE RESURRECTION OF JESUS

The best-documented 'survival' of all time must be
the resurrection of Jesus. That is why it's the single
most vital piece of evidence about life beyond death.
Whatever one's personal beliefs or convictions about
Jesus, one can't ignore the claim that this man died,
and on the third day after his death returned to life.
Balanced and intelligent people down the ages have
believed that it happened, and still do. The evidence for
and against has been exhaustively examined over the
centuries both by believers and unbelievers, because
it is correctly seen as the absolute lynch-pin of the
Christian case. Indeed, St Paul argued that 'if Christ
has not been raised, your faith is futile'.[1]

So let us look at the resurrection of Jesus Christ in
some detail, to judge the strength of the evidence for
it and to see what it does and does not say about the
more general question of life beyond death.[1]

Few people nowadays, and none at all, I think,
who are taken seriously, would deny that there was
a man called Jesus who lived in the Roman province
of Judaea in the early years of the first century AD.

His existence is not only attested by the writers of the four Gospels (who might be considered prejudiced witnesses, being Christian believers) but also by a number of distinguished non-Christian historians, including the Roman, Tacitus and the Jew, Josephus. Various archaeological finds this century have also supplied independent evidence for details and names in the Gospel accounts – the Roman officials Quirinius and Pontius Pilate, for instance, and the *gabbatha* or 'pavement' mentioned by St John.

The same sources witness to the fact that Jesus was executed under the jurisdiction of Pontius Pilate, probably in AD 30, and that his death was by crucifixion. The nature of crucifixion, and the way in which the Roman army carried it out, preclude any possibility that at the end of it he was not dead.

Yet within a few weeks the followers of Jesus were openly and boldly claiming that he had risen from the dead and that they had seen him. The accounts of these resurrection appearances as we have them in the Gospels are not identical, and to some extent they can even be seen as contradictory over details. Yet taken together they provide a convincing picture of a group of men and women – the disciples of Jesus – whose reluctance to believe in the resurrection of Jesus was overcome by the sheer irresistibility of the evidence.

As a journalist and radio producer for over thirty years, I am used to interviewing 'witnesses', and also evaluating interviews of them by other reporters. One would have a deep suspicion of a dozen or more identical stories: the whiff of collusion would be strong in the air. But these witnesses have the unmistakable ring of conviction. The disciples were convinced that they had seen Jesus alive after his death – the *real* Jesus, not a ghost or apparition. And they were prepared to stake their lives on it.

But it is not just a matter of accepting the testimony of the disciples. They claimed that the tomb of Jesus was empty – that his body had gone. That in itself is an important piece of evidence. After all, the burials of executed public agitators (which was how Jesus was seen) were not hole-in-the-corner affairs, especially when the 'agitator' had the kind of public reputation that Jesus had acquired. Not only that, but there had been talk earlier that Jesus would 'rise from the dead', so the authorities would be doubly careful that he didn't, and that his disciples couldn't claim that he had. Indeed, one of the Gospels claims that the tomb was sealed and a guard put on it, which would seem to have been sensible precautions.[2]

But the disciples found the tomb empty on that first Easter morning, and within a few weeks were saying so publicly and noisily. It should have been easy for the authorities to refute so outlandish a claim, either by producing the corpse or by demonstrating that the tomb had been robbed. Yet so far as history records the powers that be offered no rational counter to the claims of the disciples. They did not produce the body of Jesus, presumably because they couldn't. And they singularly failed to convince anyone that the body had been stolen.

In any case, the only people with any interest in stealing the body of Jesus would have been the disciples themselves. There was no market for dead bodies for medical research, and the main interest of tomb-robbers was in ornaments or fine linen buried with the body. But in the case of Jesus there were certainly no 'ornaments' – and the 'fine linen' was left behind in the tomb! So if the body wasn't taken by tomb-robbers, and wasn't removed by the authorities – who would presumably have produced it in public when the disciples started to claim Jesus had risen from the dead – then that only leaves the followers of Jesus. Could *they* have taken away the body? But if they had, then why on earth would they claim that Jesus had risen from the dead? Many of them died for that belief. Is it conceivable that they would have done so had they been responsible for stealing and then presumably hiding his body? Do those first preachers of the resurrection of Jesus sound remotely like men and women who knew it was all a hoax?

The accounts of the resurrection appearances of Jesus are not an extra detail tacked on to the end of the gospel story. They *are* the gospel story. When St Paul, writing to the church in Corinth in about AD 55 – a mere twenty-five years or so after the crucifixion – wanted to summarise the Christian message as he had received it twenty years earlier he set out a series of facts about Jesus: that he 'died for our sins', that he was buried (that is, he was really and truly dead), that he was 'raised' on the third day, and that he appeared to Peter, the twelve apostles and even to 'five hundred of the brothers at the same time'. He adds, 'Most of them are still living, though some have died.'[3] That is a bold claim, because what he is saying is that the witnesses to the risen Jesus, the people who actually saw him alive after his crucifixion, were available to be interviewed. This was not some event in remote history, a kind of distant legend, but something subject to ordinary verification.

That is the statement of a man confident of the truth of his evidence. Look, he says in effect, here is the proof that Jesus rose from the dead. He was seen at different times and places by all the twelve apostles – the chosen witnesses – and then on one occasion by five hundred people . . . and if you don't believe me, you can check it for yourself, because most of them are still alive. He was inviting sceptics in Corinth (and there were some), to put his claim to the test. There were hundreds of eye-witnesses of the resurrection. True, they were a few hundred miles away in Judaea, but they were not totally inaccessible.

Paul was presenting Christianity as it ought always to be presented – as a historical religion, rooted in certain events that actually happened, at a place on the map of the world and at a date in its history. And Christianity, preached in that way, spread like wildfire over the Roman world during the first century. There is plenty of evidence, archaeological and literary, that belief in Jesus as the Son of God risen from the dead had taken root in almost every part of the Roman Empire by about AD 70. In other words, in a single lifetime a man was born, lived, died, and became the founder of a major religion which held that he rose from the dead. This was not a peripheral belief about Jesus, something his followers could accept or reject. It *was* their message: 'Jesus and the resurrection.'

Let us be absolutely clear what this means. Within the lifetime of those who were eye-witnesses of the crucial events a religion was born and spread with amazing rapidity which claimed that its founder, executed by the Roman authorities, had risen from the dead. No amount of argument over details about the crucifixion and burial of Jesus can obscure the central fact. The Christians believed that Jesus had risen from the dead, and their opponents, both Jewish and Roman, who were desperate to disprove the claim, simply failed to do so. Unlike us, they had access to eye-witnesses. They could cross-examine them and even, given the Roman style of doing things, torture them in an effort to get them to deny their faith. They could probe for flaws, go back over records in Jerusalem, produce their own witnesses to the events of that remarkable weekend. They had the will to do it, and the motivation. By the final decades of the century Christianity was widely regarded by the authorities as a serious menace. It should not have been difficult, in those circumstances, to demolish the incredible argument that a man had come back from the dead. *Yet it was not done.* One can only deduce that this was because it simply could not be done.

It's sometimes argued that those were gullible days, quite unlike our modern world. People were ready to believe all manner of weird and wonderful legends and fantasies. Gods and goddesses popped down from heaven and popped back again. Miracles were two a penny. Without our scientific scepticism, they were unable to distinguish between what was and wasn't feasible. So the argument goes.

But this simply will not do. Quite apart from its highly idealised view of modern people, who seem perfectly willing to believe in such incredible things as flying saucers, little green men from space and astrology, it is an uninformed picture of the Graeco-Roman world of the first century.

It was not an age of gullibility, but of cynicism and scepticism. The dominant school of Greek thought, Stoicism, rejected any idea of life beyond death. So did one of the two major Jewish schools of thought, the Sadducees. There was no shortage of eloquent and learned voices ready to do battle with any religion or philosophy that proposed as its central belief that a person came back from the dead.

We can see this in the report in the book of the Acts of the Apostles of St Paul's speech to the Greek Areopagus in Athens – a kind of academic council. They listened to him attentively while he spoke of common ground – of God as the creator of all and of the unity of the human race as his offspring. But as soon as he mentioned the resurrection of Jesus, the meeting broke up. They found his claim laughable. Far from being gullibly disposed to accept it, they behaved exactly like their modern counterparts and poured scorn on the very idea.

So from two assertions which are very nearly undeniable – that Jesus of Nazareth existed in the first thirty or so years of the first century AD, and that by AD 70 the Christian religion was well established in the Roman Empire – we are able to argue the strength of the case for the resurrection of Jesus. If Jesus lived, he must have died. Yet here was a fast-growing religion, very unpopular with the authorities, which claimed that he had come back from the dead. Neither learned opposition nor vicious and bloody persecution were able to extinguish that claim. Those who wish to refute it today, nearly two thousand years after the event, must face the facts head on. Clever and powerful people in the months and years immediately following the first preaching of the Christian message did their best to discredit it . . . and they failed. There is no new evidence and the verdict must still be the same. Incredible as it seems, the most likely explanation of those strange events is that Jesus rose from the dead and was seen by his disciples. Every other explanation creates more problems than it solves.

And if Jesus rose from the dead, if a man who had been dead and buried was seen by his closest friends and talked with them, then *death is not the end*. In at least one case, a human being has come back from the other side of death to give us proof that there can be life beyond the grave. In the most public way, Jesus Christ demonstrated the truth of what he had taught: that the dead *do* 'rise again'. One man did it, and because of that we know that it is at least a possibility. What we must consider next is what the resurrection of Jesus, which is admittedly a special case, tells us about the wider question of our own possible survival beyond death.

6

WHAT KIND OF BODY?

What was it those Christian eye-witnesses of the resurrection of Jesus actually saw? It's an important question, highly relevant to our understanding of life beyond death. After all, here we have a claimed encounter not with a ghost, but with a living human being who has come back from beyond death. What was he like? Was he the same person as before, or very different? In what form did they see him? Was he 'flesh and bones', as we say, or something else? It's not enough to say simply that they saw, or met, 'Jesus'. The world is full of people who claim that! If this was really the Jesus who was born to Mary, grew up in Nazareth, preached in Galilee and died on a hill outside Jerusalem, and if he was truly alive, then their testimony is the most powerful available to us about life after death.

But *was* he the 'same' person, or had he changed in some way?

Probably the simplest approach to that question is to draw up two lists, one of the ways in which Jesus after the resurrection was different, and the other of ways in which he was the same.

Into the first list, of the dissimilarities, must go a number of pieces of eye-witness evidence which are frequently overlooked, or seized upon to support a preconceived idea of the nature of Jesus after his resurrection. For example, it is really quite undeniable that his appearance was changed, and changed to such an extent or in such a way that even his closest friends failed to recognise him. Mary of Magdala 'supposed he was the gardener' on the morning of the resurrection.[1] Two disciples walked seven miles to Emmaus with him the same day and did not recognise him until a familiar mannerism in the way he 'broke bread' for the evening meal 'opened their eyes'.[2] Less obviously, Peter and the other disciples needed, and received, other evidence than the evidence of their eyes that it was in fact Jesus who met them by the lake during their fishing expedition.

This incident is in some ways the most revealing of them all. After the resurrection, apparently slightly impatient at the delay in the arrival of the expected 'kingdom', seven of the disciples took a boat out on Lake Galilee for a night's fishing. Despite their professional skills and experience, they caught nothing. However, just as day was breaking Jesus stood on the beach and called to them. 'The disciples did not know that it was Jesus,' John recalls. The figure on the beach told them to cast their net on the starboard side of the boat. They did, and caught an enormous quantity of fish. John then shouted to Peter, 'It's the Lord!' and Peter, typically, leapt overboard and swam ashore to greet him.[3]

When the others joined them, they found that Jesus had lit a fire on the beach and they all had breakfast together. At this point John intriguingly observes, 'Now none of the disciples dared ask him, "Who are you?" They knew it was the Lord.' We may well ask, *how* did they 'know'? Clearly not by the evidence of their eyes, or they would have had no need to ask who he was. It was what had happened, the miracle of the fishes, the thoughtful act of preparing a meal – in other words, the *sort of person Jesus was* – which convinced them beyond doubt.

So I think it is obvious that the external appearance of Jesus was in some way changed, at any rate from the tortured figure they had last seen on the cross. The physical properties of his body were also changed, and very radically. He specifically denied that he was a ghost or 'spirit' (and clearly he wasn't, because he could be touched and could himself touch things). He assured them that he had 'flesh and bones', as the disciples could see. Both of those claims are in Luke's Gospel, and it seems his particular concern to emphasise the 'normality' of the risen Jesus.[4] Yet, as Luke and the other Gospel writers tell us, Jesus was apparently able to appear in places many miles apart without travelling by any recognised means, could enter rooms through locked doors, and eventually be 'taken from their sight', on the Mount of the Ascension.

It's hardly necessary to say that none of these things is feasible for a 'normal' human body, and in fact none of them happened to Jesus during his earthly life up to the time of his resurrection. Until then, he was unquestionably an ordinary human being, in the physical sense. If he did not eat, he got hungry. If he didn't drink, he got thirsty. At night he was tired and needed to sleep. If he was cut, he bled. The long journey from Galilee to Jerusalem was undertaken on foot and lasted several days – and there was never the slightest suggestion that he might travel it in any but a completely 'normal' way.

Yet after the resurrection all this was changed. There was something undeniably and fundamentally different about the body of Jesus.

St Paul said that 'Christ being raised from the dead, will never die again; death has no longer dominion over him.'[5] That in itself says something very remarkable indeed about the body of Jesus after the resurrection. All human bodies are mortal. They lie under the 'dominion' of death. As we've seen, they begin to die from the moment they're born. A body that will 'never die' is not a 'human' body, in any sense that we can use the word 'human'. Yet we are told – and those resurrection stories in the Gospels illustrate it vividly – that this 'new' body of Jesus would 'never die again'. It simply wasn't subject either to the insidious process of growing old nor to the sudden onslaught

54

of disease or accident, nor was it confined within the limits of space and time, as our bodies are.

The risen body of Jesus seemed to be living within an entirely different set of parameters, where the normal human limitations didn't apply. One is driven to conclude that it could not have been composed as ordinary bodies are. It may indeed have had 'flesh and bones', as Luke reports, but it was not limited by them in the way we are. Bars and bolts couldn't shut it out and death itself could never touch it.

Yet it was a *real* body. There can be no doubt about that. Hundreds of people couldn't have been so mistaken, especially when Jesus went out of his way to demonstrate the fact. It was like a human body, but it was not identical with our human bodies. There was clearly a continuity of life between the body of Jesus that was buried and the one that the disciples met in the upper room, but in the process of resurrection it appears to have undergone a very fundamental change. That, at least, seems obvious.

So much for the list of ways in which Jesus's body after the resurrection was different from his body before it. It had a different appearance, in some elusive way, and it had a different 'form' or constitution. It was 'like' the body of Jesus that was buried, but it was not 'identical' with it.

Now let's consider the similarities. In what ways could we say that the post-resurrection body of Jesus was the same as the one that had walked the streets of Galilee and Judaea? Strangely, they all seem to

55

come down to one factor, but that factor is so important that it outweighs all the dissimilarities. It is simply this: Jesus before and after the resurrection was undeniably *the same person*. No matter what extraordinary changes had taken place in his bodily form or capabilities, all who knew him well had no doubt at all who he was. They 'knew' it was the Lord. 'We have seen the Lord!' – not his ghost, or someone remarkably like him, but . . . *the Lord*.

How did they recognise him? How was it that, despite what are obviously major differences in his physical appearance and what we might call 'constitution', they could be so sure that this really was Jesus – so sure that they were prepared to die for it?

Mary of Magdala recognised his voice, or possibly a familiar mode of address – the way he said 'Mary'. The two disciples on the road to Emmaus recognised his mannerisms or style: the way he broke the bread. The men by the lake recognised his characteristic activity in the way he performed the miracle of the fish – and, of course, his thoughtfulness in lighting the fire and preparing breakfast. In other words, they all recognised the person, or *personality*, of a man they had known well. Whatever changes the resurrection had made to the body of Jesus, he was the same person. About that they were in no doubt, either then or at any time later.

So what we have arrived at in this examination of the resurrection of Jesus is almost exactly the same position as that suggested by all the other evidences of survival. What survives death is not 'this body' but 'this person'. St Paul said that 'flesh and blood cannot inherit the kingdom of God', and when you think about it that is obvious.[6] Bodies designed for life on this planet, in a particular set of circumstances, are not designed for life in the eternal realm with God. Whatever 'heaven' is – and we'll be looking at that question later – it is not simply this life replicated somewhere else, complete with gravity, oxygen, air pressure and so on. For a new kind of existence we need a new kind of body, and I believe that the only clues we have as to what that body will be like are the reports about the body of Jesus after his resurrection.

The personality of Jesus after his resurrection expressed itself in a new body, no longer subject to the limitations imposed on a space-time earthly body. To use Professor Mackay's analogy, the message was the same but the transmitter was new and better. To use John Houghton's analogy, the hardware had been changed, but the software had the same 'program' – though now capable of much greater things because the new hardware was better than the old one! Not only was it better in general terms (less confined, less limited, immortal) but it was also perfectly designed to live on in a spiritual environment. It was no longer really at home in this world. It all seems a perfect illustration of a rather elusive statement of Jesus, 'That which is born of the flesh is flesh, and that which is born of the Spirit is spirit.'[7]

According to the Bible, this transformation is not unique to Jesus. It is to be the pattern of all resurrection. Not immediately at death, as in the case of Jesus, but just as instantly, our bodies will be changed and we shall enter a new environment in a form perfectly suited to life there. And it will be *us*: not our ghosts or our 'souls' but the whole personality will break through the barrier of flesh and on into a new realm of living, just as it did with Jesus. This is how St Paul describes it:

> Listen, I tell you a mystery: We will not all sleep [that is, die], but we will all be changed – in a flash, in the twinkling of an eye, at the last trumpet. For the trumpet will sound, the dead will be raised imperishable, and we will be changed. For the perishable must clothe itself with the imperishable, and the mortal with immortality . . . then the saying that is written will come true: 'Death has been swallowed up in victory.'[8]

But what is the relationship between our earthly bodies and these changed 'heavenly' ones? Is there any link or connection at all, or are they completely new and different? And if they are new and different, how can there be any recognition of those we love in the life beyond death?

In a way, these questions have already been answered, if we accept the resurrection of Jesus as the 'prototype' of all resurrection from the dead. After all, the disciples – despite a few initial difficulties in some cases – all recognised Jesus. They knew who he was and in a very genuine way resumed their old relationship with him. He wasn't another person, or a remote spiritual essence, but the young man they had known and with whom they had spent the previous three years. They were absolutely clear about that, at least.

There was a very real connection between the earthly body of Jesus and his risen one, but they were not identical. One could describe the link as 'development', because that seems to describe the kind of continuity which his new body had with his previous one. The second develops out of the first – it's a refinement of it, a further stage . . . a mutation, I suppose, if you want a scientific term. The second is incomparably higher and more advanced than the first, of course. But it presents the same person. The continuity is of personality; the change is the form in which that personality presents itself. That seems to be the answer to the question of the connection or link between earthly bodies and 'heavenly' ones. The latter are new, and in some ways different, but there is a continuity of *life* between them and their predecessors that makes recognition feasible. The person is the same, but the 'form' has changed.

Flesh and blood is our present form, with the limitations that that imposes. But what is to be our 'form' in life beyond this earth?

As it happens, the Christians at Corinth back in

the first century, a mere couple of decades after the resurrection of Jesus, asked precisely that question. Here is St Paul's answer, from his first letter to them, probably written in AD 55:

> But someone may ask, 'How are the dead raised? With what kind of body will they come?' How foolish! What you sow does not come to life unless it dies. When you sow, you do not plant the body that will be, but just a seed, perhaps of wheat or of something else. But God gives it a body as he has determined, and to each kind of seed he gives its own body . . . So will it be with the resurrection of the dead. The body that is sown is perishable, it is raised imperishable; it is sown in dishonour, it is raised in glory; it is sown in weakness, it is raised in power; it is sown a natural body, it is raised a spiritual body.
>
> If there is a natural body, there is also a spiritual body. So it is written: 'The first man Adam became a living being'; the last Adam, a life-giving spirit. The spiritual did not come first, but the natural, and after that the spiritual. The first man was of the dust of the earth, the second man from heaven. As was the earthly man, so are those who are of the earth; and as is the man from heaven, so also are those who are of heaven. And just as we have borne the likeness of the earthly man, so shall we bear the likeness of the man from heaven.

I declare to you, brothers, that flesh and blood cannot inherit the kingdom of God, nor does the perishable inherit the imperishable.[9]

These words of Paul from the first century repay close study, because they express the heart of the Christian, as contrasted with the pagan, or superstitious, doctrine of immortality. There's no crude notion here of dead bodies rising from their graves or miraculously reassembling after cremation. Neither is there any suggestion that the resurrection is to some shadowy half-existence like the abodes of the dead in ancient literature. Instead, there is a profound picture of development from a simpler to a more complex form of life. The second, as we have seen, is infinitely 'better' than the first – more 'glorious', more 'splendid', more 'powerful'. You could never describe a ghost in those terms!

Paul is quite clear that our earthly bodies die. They are 'perishable', with all that that implies. Those who ridicule the whole idea of resurrection must in fairness accept that Christianity has never taught that a dead human body is anything other than 'perishable'. Bodies die and disintegrate, and that is that, so far as the physical body is concerned. 'What you sow does not come to life unless it dies', says Paul, describing what happens when a seed is planted. When the plant has fully grown, what has become of the seed itself? It has gone, disappeared, its life now part of a greater, more complex being.

And that, he argues, is what happens to our bodies at death.

And this 'second' life, the resurrection life, is on every count better. That, in its context, is the heart of Paul's argument. He uses some rather strange analogies, to modern thinking, comparing the superiority of the sun to the moon, and so on, but it all comes down to one central point: things can be comparable but distinctively different, and that spiritual life is comparable to natural life, but different *and superior*.

For the apostle, earthly life is perishable, crude and weak. Heavenly life is imperishable, glorious and powerful. Yet there is a circle of comparability. They are not two entirely different or separate things. The second (spiritual life) is an extension or development of the first (natural life). But the development is always from the lower to the higher form rather than the opposite. As we saw in the case of the resurrection of Jesus, there is a developmental relationship between the earthly body and the resurrection body, but it is a development *upwards*. At death we move to a higher, not a lower plane of existence.

Once we have really got this into our thinking our whole attitude to death will be transformed. If all we have to look forward to at death is at best extinction and at worst a vague half-existence in some twilight spirit world, then no wonder we shrink from the very thought of it. We don't enjoy the idea of ceasing to exist, but neither do normal, life-loving human beings relish relegation to a kind of sub-life, which is all that many non-Christian theories of survival amount to. The best of them, it is true, look on to some kind of blissful union with the 'ultimate', but none, it seems to me, can match the Christian emphasis on the superiority at every level and in every way of life that begins at death. It is as far superior to this one as the life of the butterfly on the wing is to that of the caterpillar on the leaf – but in both cases a transformation is required. We have to be changed in order to inherit heaven. But it is a small price to pay for the glory, splendour and joy that lie ahead of us.

That is the real 'message' of the resurrection of Jesus: the spiritual body and the spiritual life are better and more *real* than their physical predecessors. The resurrection life has everything good from this earthly life, but without the things that make it earthbound, limited and frustrating. Over everything on earth hangs the dark shadow of time. We never seem to have enough of it to do all the things we should like to do, or to become the people we ought to be. We often wish we had more time – time for those who love us, and time for God. And sometimes we long, too, to see the day – still, it seems, far off – when God's justice, mercy and peace will reign in his tortured world. This life, for all its wonders, has about it the aura of incompleteness, as though we all know that there is some better thing waiting beyond, somewhere, but always just out of our reach.

That 'better thing' is what Jesus called the kingdom of heaven, where God reigns and his will is perfectly done. We can see hints and reflections of it here and now, as people turn to him and seek to know and do his will. But it is always imperfect, incomplete – and temporary. We pray and long for God's will to be done on earth, but we know that it *is* done in heaven, and one of the joys of the life with him will be to experience life in community as he intended it to be.

'God will be with them', says the writer of Revelation in his vision of heaven. 'He will wipe every tear from their eyes. There will be no more death or mourning or crying or pain, for the old order of things has passed away.'[10] Yet in losing death, pain, tears and mourning we do not lose what is essentially human. We carry over all that is essential – the 'kernel' of the seed, in St Paul's language – but 'God gives it a body as he has chosen', and that new body is free from all of those painful limitations of human life on earth.

All of which serves to emphasise that if the Christian doctrine of resurrection is true – and I have tried to show how strong and convincing it is when properly understood – then there is no need for distaste, fear or trepidation in the face of death. What lies beyond, for those who are raised with Christ, is superbly good. The God who made this earth so splendid, with its wonderful variety of colour and form, its joys of human love, family, creativity and community and its magnificence in art, music and literature, has promised that the next life will be 'more glorious'. What could anyone ask more than that?

7

WHAT IS HEAVEN LIKE?

Not surprisingly, people often ask what heaven is like. They're probably more disappointed than surprised to be told that no-one knows – no-one on earth, that is. With the best will in the world it's not possible to give an honest and accurate answer, though there will be those who are prepared to try.

There are two different reasons for the difficulty, and both are fairly obvious. The first is that there is an acute shortage of people who have been there – at any rate, people with whom we can communicate. The second is that by its very nature heaven is going to be unlike anything we have ever known. Imagine trying to explain to an unborn baby what a modern city is like, or jet travel, and you will begin to appreciate the problem. But at least the baby in the womb is living in our space-time situation, is part of our earth environment and is subject to the same physical laws as the rest of us. But heaven is beyond all of those: beyond earth, beyond space and time and beyond the physical laws of the universe. In other words, whatever heaven is, it must be *fundamentally* different.

So, deprived of all those elements which enable us to describe anything in normal terms, it's not surprising that the Bible confines itself to saying what heaven is 'like' – comparisons, analogies – rather than what it is *like*, if you see what I mean. In fact, Jesus, who spoke more about heaven than anyone else in the Bible, did so almost entirely in similes and metaphors. 'The kingdom of heaven is like . . .'

But perhaps we should start by saying what heaven is *not*, because distortions and caricatures of the biblical picture of heaven have led many intelligent people to reject the whole idea as childish and pre-scientific. Some Christian apologists have fallen into the same trap, I feel. Back in the 1960s John Robinson, in his influential book *Honest to God*, argued that 'man come of age' could never be expected to accept the idea of a heaven 'up in the skies'. Dr Robinson, an outstanding New Testament scholar, was aware that only the most woodenly literalistic interpretation of the Scriptures could be understood as describing heaven in such terms. Of course the ancient world did think in terms of a 'three-decker' universe, with the 'heavens' – the sky – as the dwelling place of God, so it was quite natural that people should think of heaven as 'up there'.

But in fact Jesus never spoke of heaven in spatial terms. 'Heaven', in his teaching, was 'eternal life' or the 'kingdom of God' – states of being in relation to God rather than a 'place' in the space-time sense of the word. In rejecting, justifiably, the language of some Victorian hymn writers ('There's a home for little children/Above the bright blue sky . . .') it would be foolish to reject the consistent, satisfying and beautiful picture of heaven provided for us by Jesus and the New Testament writers. The marvellous imagery of the book of Revelation was never intended to be read as a factual description of heaven, any more than its Four Horsemen of the Apocalypse are meant to be taken as actual historical figures. Allegorical and metaphorical language cannot be treated in such an unimaginative way if we wish to uncover its true and deepest meaning.

For instance, heaven is not 'up'. I realise that will come as a surprise to many people, because if an idea is old enough, no matter how flimsy its basis, it's hard to eradicate it. Not only that, but a great deal of biblical language seems to support it – the very term 'ascension' to describe the return of Jesus to heaven has obvious connections with the idea of 'going up'.

At the same time, other biblical pictures seem to contradict that idea. In the opening of the magnificent twenty-first chapter of Revelation, for example, we read this: 'Then I saw a new heaven and a new earth, for the first heaven and the first earth had passed away, and there was no longer any sea. I saw the Holy City, the new Jerusalem, *coming down* [my italics] out of heaven from God, prepared as a bride beautifully dressed for her husband. And I heard a loud voice from the throne saying, "Now the dwelling of God is with men" . . .'[1]

However you read this, you can't take it in a crudely literal way! It would seem that the 'new heaven and earth', where God dwells, the 'holy city, new Jerusalem', comes *down*, though in fact all such spatial ideas are irrelevant to a 'place' which is not in a space-time environment at all. The important thing is that heaven is where God is, and in this 'new' heaven God has drawn his people into a new community centred around him. In that community tears will be wiped away and sorrow, pain and death will be abolished: 'for the former things are passed away'.

So although heaven is not 'up' in strictly literal terms, 'up' is a very good way to describe something which is vastly superior to that which it replaces. We often use the word in that sense – she's gone 'up' to Oxford, he's made his way 'up' through the firm, they've developed 'higher' skills. In none of these cases do we literally mean 'upwards', but simply superior or better. And heaven is most certainly 'up' in that sense. It is infinitely 'above' anything we know.

So heaven is not 'up' geographically – after all, what is 'up' in Australia is, strictly, 'down' in Europe. But even if it is not 'up there' or even 'out there', in the literal sense, it *is* greatly superior to anything we have known on earth, 'higher' and better. To think of heaven as though it were simply another 'place', like Mars or Alpha Centauri, is to diminish it. Christians are not defending the idea of some dark or hidden corner of the universe where we imagine heaven may be located. Heaven is not in a corner anywhere and it will never be located by even the most powerful radio telescopes. It is simply not in their world: up, down or sideways.

Neither is heaven a matter of pearly gates, golden streets and the sound of harps, though all of these are in the picture of heaven in John's great vision of the future in Revelation. In the language of apocalyptic literature (in which the book of Revelation is written), these simply represented the ultimate in splendour, beauty and enjoyment. Modern British people might speak of a land of endless sunshine without meaning anything more than an idyllic holiday haunt. 'Heaven' is no more made of gold and precious stones than the promised land of Canaan literally 'flowed with milk and honey', but the *idea* being conveyed in both cases is clear enough to the reader with a bit of imagination.

Heaven does not 'go on for ever and ever', in the sense that it occupies vast aeons of time stretching away into eternity. Many people have told me that they would sooner cease to exist at death than spend eternity 'playing harps'. There's something decidedly unattractive to human minds about the idea of anything going on for ever and ever. 'I'd be bored stiff,' people say. 'After a few thousand years you'd have done it all, but there'd still be endless time to come.' They make heaven sound like a wet weekend in Wigan.

G. R. Evans has dealt with this objection:

To modern eyes heaven seems beautiful but dull. This conception of sameness as tedious is a relatively modern one. It depends on our idea of time. Boredom requires longish stretches of time to take hold. We should not think of heaven as being in one place for endless 'time'. We should be envisaging a freedom from the confinement of time and space which will make it possible for us to be with all our friends at once and individually, to be enjoying an infinite variety of things as we choose, without delay or hurry, crowding or isolation. It is something new, a new quality of life.

In fact, as I've tried to show, the whole notion of time as well as space is quite irrelevant to heaven. Just as heaven has no location in space – you can't find it on any map of the universe – so it has no location in time either. It is not 'in' time any more than it is 'in' space. The whole idea of measuring years in heaven is like trying to measure love with a ruler. It's simply not capable of that kind of definition.

Heaven is where God is, and heaven is *when* God is, too. And God is eternal. That's not the same thing as saying that God lasts for ever, though some of our religious language might give that impression (for example, 'for ever and ever, Amen'). An 'eternal' being is not part of our space-time system and so cannot be defined in its very limited terms. God has no beginning and no end. He simply *exists*. Human beings were, are or will be according to the rules of time and space. God *is*. He was never younger than he is now, and he does not grow old. And that is what heaven is like. There will be no tenses there – no past and future, at any rate, but one permanently present tense.

Of course, that's a very difficult idea to get hold of for all of us, because it is totally beyond our present experience. Yet a moment's thought will confirm that a 'God' who is *not* eternal, in this sense, is no 'God' at all, but a temporal being like we are. If there was a time when God did not exist, then at some point he came into existence and is a dependent being like his creatures. The real answer to the child's question, 'But who made God?' *has* to be 'God', because if he was 'made' he is not, by definition, God at all but a creature like ourselves.

Equally, if there were to be a time when God ceased to exist then he is as captive to mortality as we are, and presumably all that he has brought into being will disappear with him. By definition (again), God is self-existent, depending on no-one else and the ultimate source of all being. As soon as we use the word 'God' we have to accept that it must refer to a self-existent being, or we are emptying it of any distinctive meaning at all. Life in heaven is life *with* God and life *in* God, and that must mean life as he lives it, free of the limitations of time and space: *eternal* life, as the Bible calls it.

So – what *is* heaven like?

Having looked at some of the things heaven is not, we might now try to answer the question as to what it is. In fact, the negatives have already provided some of the answers. If heaven is not located in time and space,

71

then it is an entirely different mode of existence from any we have ever known or could imagine. It is literally beyond our comprehension, as God himself is.

But that doesn't mean that the Bible offers no clues to what heaven is like. One has been mentioned already: heaven is where God is (and hell, it seems to follow, is where God is not – an appalling concept). So heaven is in many respects like God: personal, eternal, good, true and beautiful. That doesn't mean, however, that it is just a series of abstract qualities, any more than God is. Heaven is a mode of living, where relationships are important and where we can all develop a greater insight into what is true and experience love as never before. 'Then [i.e. in heaven] I shall *know*, as I am now known', writes St Paul. 'Love never fails.'[2]

The 'heavens' of some religions in the past, such as the *Valhalla* of the Norsemen or the Elysian Fields of the Romans, are really little more than glamorised recreations of life on earth. At the other extreme, the 'heaven' of some eastern religions, like *Nirvana*, are little more than spiritualised concepts – they hardly involve 'living' in any ordinary sense of the word.

The Christian heaven avoids both these extremes. It is not just a 'second innings' (on a better wicket, of course!), like our present life but with the bumps and handicaps taken out. But neither is it simply a concept. In heaven we live more fully and satisfyingly than ever before – what Jesus called 'life in all its fullness'.[3] That life involves all the really important elements of what we now enjoy: relationships, development, knowledge,

communication and love. And all experienced in the
same mode as life on earth – personality expressed
through a body.

The differences compared to earthly life will be
enormous, as we should expect. But they will enhance
rather than diminish our experience of living. We shall
recognise our loved ones, because they too will be
'personalities expressed through a body'. But that
recognition will be by who they are rather than by
what they look like. We shall know them with a depth
and insight and love we have never experienced before.
Life – and love – will be transformed in the presence
of its creator and sustainer.

Perhaps one should add here a word of caution
against the exclusively individualistic idea of heaven
that is sometimes popularised in hymns and songs –
'I've got a mansion in the sky' . . . 'I want to be in
their number, when the saints go marching in.' While
it is true that we shall be individual persons in heaven,
heaven itself is a fellowship or communion centred on
God, not on our personal desires or preferences. And
God is selfless, self-sacrificing *love*. That suggests that
at the heart of heaven is not the fulfilment of our
own wishes but the perfect expression of the will of
God, which is itself pure love.[4] Our joy in heaven, in
other words, will not be a private, selfish one but a
marvellous shared experience of love in its fullness.

Alongside this wonderful picture offered to us by
the writers of the Bible and by Jesus Christ himself,
most of the common questions raised about heaven

begin to look rather threadbare. Will there be animals in heaven? Will people speak English, or German, or Italian ... or Latin, perhaps? What age will we be in heaven? How can heaven be large enough to contain all the people who have ever lived and died? And so on.

The answer to them all is really the same. Because heaven cannot be converted into space-time terminology, there are simply no words or pictures available to us that are adequate to convey its properties to human, earthly minds. This may seem rather inadequate as an answer, but it's the truth. If there is a heaven at all, then almost by definition it must be beyond our comprehension. Until we get there, we shall probably have to be content to believe that the God who made this passing world so beautiful and richly satisfying is more than able to make the next one even better.

The life 'beyond' is linked with this life. That is the central and fundamental truth about it. It develops from it. Human personality flowers there into its finest and most wonderful form, which is in fact the character of Christ. This is how the first Epistle of John puts it: 'We are God's children now; it does not yet appear what we shall be, but we know that when he appears we shall be like him, for we shall see him as he is.'[5]

That is what human destiny is – to be 'like Christ'. Not Christ limited, as he was on earth, by the confines of time and flesh, but Christ risen, the great, free, timeless Christ of Easter morning. That, in a sentence, is what we shall be like in heaven. And a community of people like that is what heaven will be.

8

WHO GOES THERE?

At this point the perceptive reader might well observe
that all of that seems very pleasant, but does *everybody*
go to heaven? I must admit that it's a question I have
carefully avoided up to this point. Most people are
aware that not only Christianity, but all the other
major religions, hold out the prospect of a life of
bliss after this one, but restrict it to what we might
call 'deserving' cases. Heaven, in other words, is
by selection. It is not a universal and unqualified
benefit.

But on what grounds could a fair selection be made?
Obviously that question has been raised over and
over again throughout human history. Surprisingly,
virtually every known religion has plumped for what is,
on the face of it, the least attractive notion – that entry
to heaven is by divine selection, and that the selection
is determined on grounds of moral excellence.

There could be some quite disreputable reasons for
this, of course. The threat of a judgment after death
upon the results of which depend one's future bliss or
misery is a powerful incentive to obedience on earth.

All through history religious leaders have found it difficult to resist the temptation to use it as a means of recruiting and then brow-beating their followers. 'Do what we say, and you will go to heaven. Disobey, and go to hell (or whatever preferred brand of punishment the religion has opted for).'

More reputably, the hope of heaven and the fear of hell has spurred people on to greater effort and self-discipline. It has shaped lives of sacrifice, poverty and service. It has also, it has to be said, emptied the purses and filled the temple coffers of many an unscrupulous high priest.

Yet the fact that the concept of judgment after death has been appallingly abused by some, and distorted by others, doesn't of itself disprove its reality. The fact remains that all through recorded human history most people have believed in it, in one way or another. And that is, of itself, *prima facie* evidence for an element of truth, or at least psychological need, in the idea. If a belief is as widespread – almost universal – as this, one must assume that it has some roots in reality. It is true that there are, and have always been, religions that preach Universalism – that everyone will end up in 'heaven', whatever their behaviour on earth – but they are exceptional.

There is one strong and rational argument for the idea of judgment after death which I find very persuasive. It depends on two basic premises: that God exists, and that he is good. If he doesn't exist, or if he is morally neutral or even evil, then there is plainly no reason for believing in any kind of ultimate moral judgment. But if those two premises are accepted, then the logic of the case for an ultimate judgment is strong.

After all, this life is manifestly unjust. The good suffer, the innocent are exploited, the meek are terrorised, the poor are robbed even of what they have. On the other hand, the evil often seem to flourish, the selfish make fortunes, the brutal oppress the weak and the rich get richer. Tyrants die peacefully in their beds while saints expire in agony on the rack or pyre. Of course, there are exceptions. Possibly the evil are no happier in their circumstances than the good. But clearly there is no general justice. Massive injustices go unpunished while saintly self-denial goes unrewarded.

The instinct of justice is very strong in all of us. Almost the first whole sentence a child learns is 'It's not fair!' We all constantly appeal to some abstract principle of justice whose existence we assume and which we also assume to be accepted by everyone else. Communists, atheists, humanists all make the same appeal: 'It's not *fair!*'

Yet we all know that, in the final analysis, this life is *not* fair. With the best intentions in the world, human justice is fallible. With the worst intentions – with a Hitler or Stalin, for example – injustice becomes monumental.

Now if, as we are assuming, there is a God and he is good, how can he possibly allow this state of affairs? If he does nothing, either now or after this life, to redress such gross injustice and put down such rampant evil, then he is either not God (because he lacks the *power* to do it) or he is not good (because he lacks the *will* to do it). But if he is both all-powerful and good – which is what the word 'God' means to most of us – then it seems to me he *must* act to put things right. Justice on a cosmic scale must be done, and must be seen to be done, or God is not God.

Clearly God has not yet done this on earth. We may long and pray for it, but we have not seen his perfect justice applied to the life of our world. The strong presumption, then, is that he will do it after this life is over. And that is exactly what the Bible teaches. The Letter to the Hebrews puts it like this: 'Man is destined to die once, and after that to face judgment.'[1] And that theme – of the final judgment of God, in which the mighty are put down from their thrones, the proud in their inmost hearts scattered to the four winds, the rich sent away empty and the poor lifted up – runs right through the teaching of Jesus and the apostles. It might seem that God is blind to human injustice, but one day it will be seen that he cares intensely about it and delays only to give people time to change their ways. When that day comes, he will act in divine power to put right the inequalities and evils of life on earth.

A vital part of this process is the judgment of the individual after death.[2] There are many pictures of this in the New Testament but the most persistent one is of a seat of heavenly judgment from which

Jesus himself, by God's appointment, will judge the nations of the earth.[3] This is only a picture, of course, but it is a vivid and disturbing one. However much it may offend liberal sentiment, there can be no doubt at all that Jesus believed and taught that there was a very real possibility of people being excluded from heaven. The idea is there in the core of the Gospel material, among the sayings of Jesus which are accepted as representing the heart of his message.

Why should a God of love, and a Saviour sent by him to demonstrate the full extent of that love, even contemplate barring his creatures – objects of his love – from the joy of heaven? The answer is quite uncomplicated, really. Heaven, as the Bible describes it, is a community of total goodness, where people live in the presence of God. To allow evil into heaven would be like tossing a bad apple into a barrel of good ones: the place would no longer be totally good – indeed little different from what we have experienced on earth. All impurity and sin is to be excluded from heaven *simply so that it may be heaven.* 'Nothing unclean shall enter it', says the seer of Revelation, 'nor anyone who practises abomination or falsehood, but only those who are written in the Lamb's book of life.'[4]

Who can possibly qualify?

In the light of all this we may well ask, who can possibly hope to enter heaven? Surely there's no human being so perfect that they could live in a community of tota holiness and goodness without spoiling it? It would seem that God is going to be very lonely, sitting there in the isolation of his holiness, while all his squabbling, fallible, morally imperfect creatures are excluded from this new kind of 'Holy Club'.

But the last phrase of that verse from Revelation just quoted offers an answer. It is those whose names are 'written in the Lamb's book of life' who are entitled to enter heaven. So, who are they? The same book tells us. They are members of 'a great multitude that no-one could count, from every nation, tribe, people and language . . . [who] have washed their robes and made them white in the blood of the Lamb'.[5]

The 'Lamb' referred to is Jesus Christ (the 'Lamb of God', in the terminology of John's Gospel) and his 'blood' refers to the sacrifice of himself made when he died on the cross. Through that sacrifice, Christians believe, our sins can be forgiven and we can be accepted by God. In the peculiar imagery of Revelation the names of those who are forgiven and accepted in this way (those who have 'washed their robes in the blood of the Lamb') are written in the book of life. They will be admitted to heaven not because they are perfect, or lived blameless lives, but because they have been forgiven. Their 'robes' are not stained with sin, but 'white'.

That is, in essence, the Christian gospel. Forgiveness through Jesus Christ is the sure way to eternal life. It is God's way of keeping heaven holy and yet admitting to it people no better than we are. So the short answer to the question 'Who can possibly qualify for heaven?' is: 'Those who have been forgiven their sins through the sacrifice of Jesus Christ.' As I say, that's the short answer, but in truth it answers one question while raising several others!

For example, what about those who have never heard of Jesus Christ? What about the countless millions who have sincerely followed other religions and tried to lead the good life? What about all those who lived in the centuries before the coming of Jesus Christ? Are all of those to be excluded? And, if they are, what does that make of the Christian doctrine of a God of infinite love and mercy?

Those are not new questions, of course. In fact, St Paul dealt with them in his letter to the church in Rome twenty years or so after the resurrection of Jesus. He was considering the position of the 'Gentiles' – that is, people who knew nothing of God's law revealed to Israel or, at this point, anything about the Messiah, Jesus. In other words, they stand in much the same position as those who follow other religions today, or those who lived before the birth of Jesus, or through no fault of their own have never heard of him. This is what he wrote in the second chapter of Romans (from verse 14):

Indeed, when Gentiles, who do not have the law, do by nature the things required by the law, they are a law for themselves, even though they do not have the law, since they show that the requirements of the law are written on their hearts, their consciences also bearing witness, and their thoughts now accusing, now even defending them. This will take place on the day when God will judge men's secrets through Jesus Christ, as my gospel declares.

The argument is admittedly a bit tortuous, but the central point seems clear enough. Those who do not have knowledge of God's requirements will not be arbitrarily rejected, but judged – 'through Jesus Christ', the world's Saviour – according to the extent to which they have obeyed the promptings of conscience. That is emphatically *not* an easy alternative to the way of faith and forgiveness which the Christian gospel offers, but it is a way of mercy. No-one, in the final analysis, will be able to charge the 'Judge of all the earth' with injustice.

So the doors of heaven are pretty broad. At least, that's how I read the teaching of the Bible. 'God is not willing that any should perish, but that all should come to repentance.'[6] 'Christ died for our sins, and not for our sins only, but for the sins of the whole world.'[7] If people are finally excluded from the presence of God, it will not be for lack of effort on God's part! It is wilful rejection or wilful disobedience that leads to the exclusion – and to eliminate that would require that human beings ceased to be free moral agents. We have the appalling right to choose to reject God. One can only hope and assume that not many would be so crass as to employ it.

Conversely, I believe that the doors of hell are very narrow. There is not much about 'hell' in the New Testament, and almost all that there is came from the lips of Jesus himself. He referred to it as *gehenna*, which is the Hebrew word for the valley of Hinnom, just outside Jerusalem. In the time of Jesus this was the city's refuse dump, where the rubbish was burned. It was said that the smoke of its fires rose into the sky day and night. From that it's easy to see how the image of hell fire came into being.

But in fact they were fires of *cleansing* rather than punishment. *Gehenna* was a place where corruption and decay were finally destroyed. This idea is picked up in the imagery of the book of Revelation, with its picture of the lake of fire which is the 'second death', reserved for 'the devil and his angels'. However one chooses to understand this, it clearly teaches that God's purpose is the ultimate annihilation of all that is evil and corrupt from his creation. That, for me, is the positive way to think about 'hell'. In the end, God's kingdom will come and his will be done. Were it not so, then evil would have triumphed.

When shall we enter heaven?

Do people enter heaven at the moment of death, or at some future 'Day of Judgment'? That is a question which seems to trouble some people. Are we right to say of a loved one who has died, 'They're now in the presence of God'? or would it be more correct to say that they are now 'asleep' awaiting the final judgment? Whole books have been written in the past arguing this and that case, and I dare say people have been thrown out of pulpits and churches for teaching the 'wrong' thing. As with most controversies of this kind, it seems as though the Bible can be quoted on both sides. Jesus told the penitent thief on the cross that he would be with him 'today' in 'paradise'. On the other hand, St Paul seems to teach equally clearly that we shall 'all sleep' until the moment when we are 'changed, in the twinkling of an eye, at the last trumpet', to face the day of judgment.

At the risk of upsetting all those who enjoy such exercises in splitting theological hairs, I should want to say that this particular dispute seems to me totally irrelevant. If, as we have argued, the whole notion of time is meaningless in the spiritual world, then even to discuss – let alone argue over – intervals of time in the existence beyond death seems quite futile. The Bible tells us that with God 'a day is as a thousand years and a thousand years is as a day',[8] which is a rather more poetic way of saying the same thing. The 'time' taken for the metamorphosis from the physical to the spiritual world is, as we've seen, 'the twinkling of an eye'. When the final judgment comes, St Paul tells us, 'those who are alive at the time will not precede those who have fallen asleep' (that is, died).[9] All will be raised together in one instant of time, with no conscious elapsing of time between the individual moments of their deaths and the moment of resurrection. And at that moment, as I understand it, all of those forgiven and accepted by God will 'enter' heaven.

Yet, in fact, 'enter' is the wrong word. Heaven is not a 'place', in the ordinary sense of the word, but a completely new mode of existence. It is more a matter of being there than going there. Although it makes a lovely picture, I think we can dismiss ideas of the soul winging its way through the void of space to some distant celestial destination. The journey is not a natural or physical one, but a spiritual one.

That does not mean that it is less 'real'. It is one of the most obstinate of human convictions that physical equals real and spiritual equals unreal, whereas eternity will reveal that the truth is the precise opposite. Physical existence is temporary and transitory; spiritual existence is eternal and unchanging. Physical life is susceptible to decay and death. Spiritual life is gloriously free from both. The 'journey' from earth to heaven is in a very real sense an internal one, as we are transformed from the state of mind that is at enmity against God's will to a state of mind that is at one with it. It's not so much that we have to go to heaven as that heaven should come to us. In the teaching of Jesus 'eternal life' begins now, by an inner conversion of the mind and spirit, and then reaches its fulfilment in the life beyond death.

That is probably the greatest single truth about life

beyond death: that it can begin now. Eternal life can seep back into earthly life like the rising tide filling the dry pools many miles inland. That is how the great saints and mystics have lived, with eternity already in their hearts. And that is, I believe, the experience that comes to many, many people during a terminal illness. Relatives and friends observe a new serenity and calmness, often remarking how 'brave' the patient is being. In fact they are being secretly supplied from the world of the spirit which is preparing them for the final journey.

Indeed, those who have begun a life 'in Christ' on earth find the transition between the two worlds so easy as to be almost imperceptible. Many witnesses confirm this – of the joy and even eagerness with which those who have lived close to God on earth face the prospect of an even closer relationship with him in heaven. St Paul testified to it in his own experience, writing to the church at Philippi from a prison cell when what he anticipated was imminent execution: 'For to me, to live is Christ and to die is gain . . . I desire to depart and be with Christ, which is better by far . . .'[10]

When the writer and broadcaster Malcolm Muggeridge became aware of the onset of old age, he related much the same experience as St Paul – though I doubt whether the apostle would have described the choice between earthly life and heaven as a 'toss-up'!

I often wake up in the night and feel myself in some curious way, half in and half out of my body, so that I seem to be hovering between the battered old carcass that I can see between the sheets and seeing in the darkness and in the distance a glow in the sky, the lights of Augustine's City of God. In that condition, when it seems just a toss-up whether I return into my body to live out another day, or make off, there are two particular conclusions, two extraordinarily sharp impressions that come to me. The first is of the incredible beauty of our earth – its colours and shapes, its smells and its features; of the enchantment of human love and companionship, and of the blessed fulfilment provided by human work and human procreation. And the second, a certainty surpassing all words and thoughts, that as an infinitesimal particle of God's creation, I am a participant in his purposes, which are loving and not malign, creative and not destructive, orderly and not chaotic, universal and not particular. And in that certainty, a great peace and a great joy.

That 'peace' and 'joy' often seem to transform the actual experience of dying. In his book *Life Begins at Death* the late Leslie Weatherhead quotes a physician to the royal family as saying when he was dying, 'If I had the strength to hold a pen I would tell mankind what a wonderful thing it is to die.' Doctors and nurses bear this out. Far from dying in terror or anxiety, most patients achieve a calm, almost a divine serenity, at the last. Of course, in the modern world most people die following a state of unconsciousness, perhaps in a coma or deeply sedated. Yet even in that state it is not uncommon for someone to have a moment of lucidity near the end, in which they express confidence and even joy. Leslie Weatherhead speaks of one dying man who felt that his hand was being gripped too tightly: 'Don't hold me back,' he said. 'It's marvellous.'

Of course, it's tempting to try to decorate the whole business of dying with a kind of religious after-glow, and there's no denying that it can be both painful and undignified in some circumstances. But the fact remains that many people seem to have experienced at or near the moment of death some transforming inner strength, and I don't think it is fanciful to see in these occurrences evidence of heaven 'invading' the territory of earth to prepare the traveller for the journey. It seems appropriate to recall the words of Jesus to his disciples just before his own death. 'Do not let your hearts be troubled,' he said. 'Trust in God; trust also in me. In my Father's house are many rooms; if it were not so, I would have told you. I am going there to prepare a place for you.'[11]

I have often stood on the cliffs near Fishguard and watched the Irish ferry set out on its journey. Slowly it makes its way out to sea, eventually disappearing over the horizon. When it disappears, I don't assume that it has ceased to exist, along with its passengers and crew. It has simply ceased to exist in my experience, at that moment. The ship itself, of course, is still making its way across the Irish Sea and will eventually dock at Rosslare at the end of its journey.

In much the same way, death is not the end. Our loved ones have not ceased to exist when they slip across the horizon which we call death. All they have done is cease to be present in my experience of this life, at this moment of time. For them, the journey continues, and will only be complete when they stand in the presence of God in the inexpressible joy of heaven.

Death is not the end. It is not the end of life or love or beauty. It is not the end of anything good, worthwhile or lovely. And it is not the end of those we love, or of our own spiritual and moral development. There is a lot more living to be done, after this.

Beyond that horizon lies so much more; hidden from our eyes at present, but revealed in part to our minds and hearts by faith, and through the words of the Scriptures. Death is not the final enemy of the human race. That is evil. Death is the final enemy of our final enemy. Beyond it lies a new kind of life, where evil has no place at all.

APPENDIX I

BIBLICAL PASSAGES CITED

Chapter 2: 'What Happens When I Die?'

1. 'The dust returns to the ground it came from, and the spirit returns to God who gave it' (Eccles. 12:7).
2. ' "I know that my Redeemer lives, and that in the end he will stand upon the earth. And after my skin has been destroyed, yet in [or, apart from] my flesh I will see God" ' (Job 19:25, 26 text and margin). The New Revised Standard Version notes: 'The meaning of the Hebrew of this verse is uncertain.'

Chapter 3: Self, Spirit, Soul

1. 'God said to Moses, "I am who I am . . . This is my name for ever, the name by which I am to be remembered from generation to generation" ' (Exod. 3:14, 15b).
2. 'So God created man in his own image, in the image of God he created him; male and female he created them' (Gen. 1:27).

Chapter 4: Evidence for Survival

1. ' "Do not turn to mediums or seek out spiritists, for you will be defiled by them. I am the Lord your God" ' (Lev. 19:31).

Chapter 5: The Resurrection of Jesus

1. 'And if Christ has not been raised, your faith is futile; you are still in your sins . . . If only for this life we have hope in Christ, we are to be pitied more than all men' (1 Cor. 15:17, 19).
2. ' "Take a guard," Pilate answered. "Go, make the tomb as secure as you know how." So they went and made the tomb secure by putting a seal on the stone and posting a guard' (Matt. 27:65–6).
3. 'For what I received I passed on to you as of first importance: that Christ died for our sins according to the Scriptures, that he was buried, that he was raised on the third day according to the Scriptures, and that he appeared to Peter, and then to the Twelve. After that, he appeared to more than five hundred of the brothers at the same time, most of whom are still living, though some have fallen asleep' (1 Cor. 15:3–6).

Chapter 6: What Kind of Body?

1. 'Then the disciples went back to their homes, but Mary stood outside the tomb crying. As she wept, she bent over to look into the tomb and saw two angels in white, seated where Jesus' body had been, one at the head and the other at the foot. They asked her, "Woman, why are you crying?" "They have taken my Lord away," she said, "and I don't know where they have put him." At this, she turned round and saw Jesus standing there, but she did not realise that it was Jesus.

   ' "Woman," he said, "why are you crying? Who is it you are looking for?" Thinking he was the gardener, she said, "Sir, if you have carried him away, tell me where you have put him, and I will get him."

   'Jesus said to her, "Mary." She turned towards him and cried out in Aramaic, "Rabboni!" (which means Teacher). Jesus said, "Do not hold on to me, for I have not yet returned to the Father. Go instead to my brothers and tell them, "I am returning to my Father and your Father, to my God and your God."

'Mary of Magdala went to the disciples with the news: "I have seen the Lord!" ' (John 20:10–18).

2. 'As they approached the village to which they were going, Jesus acted as if he were going further. But they urged him strongly, "Stay with us, for it is nearly evening; the day is almost over." So he went in to stay with them. When he was at the table with them, he took bread, gave thanks, broke it and began to give it to them. Then their eyes were opened and they recognised him, and he disappeared from their sight' (Luke 24:28–31).

3. 'Afterwards Jesus appeared again to his disciples, by the Sea of Tiberias ... Early in the morning, Jesus stood on the shore, but the disciples did not realise that it was Jesus. He called out to them, "Friends, haven't you any fish?" "No," they answered. He said, "Throw your net on the right side of the boat and you will find some." When they did, they were unable to haul the net in because of the large number of fish. Then the disciple whom Jesus loved said to Peter, "It is the Lord!" ... When they landed, they saw a fire of burning coals there with fish on it, and some bread ... Jesus said to them, "Come and have breakfast." None of the disciples dared to ask him, "Who are you?" They knew it was the Lord' (John 21:1, 4–7, 9, 12).

4. '[Jesus said] "Look at my hands and my feet. It is I myself! Touch me and see; a ghost does not have flesh and bones, as you can see I have" ' (Luke 24:39).

5. 'For we know that since Christ was raised from the dead, he cannot die again; death no longer has mastery over him' (Rom. 6:9).

6. 'I declare to you, brothers, that flesh and blood cannot inherit the kingdom of God, nor does the perishable inherit the imperishable. Listen, I tell you a mystery: We will not all sleep, but we will all be changed – in a flash, in the twinkling of an eye, at the last trumpet' (1 Cor. 15:50).

7. '[Jesus said] "Flesh gives birth to flesh, but the Spirit gives birth to spirit" ' (John 3:6).

8. 1 Corinthians 15:51–4.

9. 1 Corinthians: 15:35–50.
10. ' "They will be his people, and God himself will be with them and be their God. He will wipe every tear from their eyes. There will be no more death or mourning or crying or pain, for the old order of things has passed away" ' (Rev. 21:3b–4).

Chapter 7: What is Heaven Like?

1. Revelation 21:1–3.
2. 'Love never fails . . . Now I know in part; then I shall know fully, even as I am fully known. And now these three remain: faith, hope and love. But the greatest of these is love' (1 Cor. 13:8a, 12b, 13).
3. '[Jesus said,] "I have come that they may have life, and have it to the full" ' (John 10:10).
4. 'God is love. Whoever lives in love lives in God, and God in him' (1 John 4:16).
5. 'Dear friends, now we are the children of God, and what we will be has not yet been made known. But we know that when he appears, we shall be like him, for we shall see him as he is' (1 John 3:2). The quote on p. 74 is from the RSV.

The passage by G. R. Evans on p. 69 is quoted by John Young in his book *Know Your Faith* (Hodder & Stoughton, 1991).

Chapter 8: Who Goes There?

1. 'Man is destined to die once, and after that to face judgment' (Heb. 9:27).
2. 'For we will all stand before God's judgment seat . . . So then, each of us will give an account of himself to God' (Rom. 14:10b, 12).
3. 'Moreover, the Father judges no-one, but has entrusted all judgment to the Son' (John 5:22).
4. 'Nothing impure will ever enter it [the city of God], nor will

anyone who does what is shameful or deceitful, but only those whose names are written in the Lamb's book of life' (Rev. 21:27).

5. 'After this I looked and there before me was a great multitude that no-one could count, from every nation, tribe, people and language, standing before the throne and in front of the Lamb. They were wearing white robes and were holding palm branches in their hands' (Rev. 7:9).

6. '[God] is patient with you, not wanting anyone to perish, but everyone to come to repentance' (2 Pet. 3:9).

7. 'He [Christ] is the atoning sacrifice for our sins, and not only for ours but also for the sins of the whole world' (1 John 2:2).

8. 'With the Lord a day is like a thousand years, and a thousand years like a day' (2 Pet. 3:8).

9. 'According to the Lord's own word, we tell you that we who are still alive, who are left till the coming of the Lord, will certainly not precede those who have fallen asleep. For the Lord himself will come down from heaven, with a loud command, with the voice of the archangel and with the trumpet call of God, and the dead in Christ will rise first. After that, we who are still alive and are left will be caught up together with them in the clouds to meet the Lord in the air. And so we will be with the Lord for ever' (1 Thess. 4:15–17).

10. 'For to me, to live is Christ and to die is gain . . . I am torn between the two: I desire to depart and be with Christ, which is better by far' (Phil. 1:21, 23).

11. '[Jesus said,] "Do not let your hearts be troubled. Trust in God; trust also in me. In my Father's house are many rooms; if it were not so, I would have told you. I am going there to prepare a place for you. And if I go and prepare a place for you, I will come back and take you to be with me that you also may be where I am' (John 14:1–3).

APPENDIX II

BOOKS AND OTHER SOURCES CITED

A. Godin (ed.), *Death and Presence (The Psychology of Death and the After-life)* (Lumen Vitae Press, Brussels, 1972), p. 69 cited.

Dr Keith Hearne, 'At Death's Door,' *Nursing Mirror,* November 18, 1981.

John Houghton, *The Search for God: Can Science Help?* (Lion, 1995). Especially chapter 9, 'A Fifth Dimension' and chapter 13, 'Natural or Supernatural?'.

Roy Lawrence, *Invitation to Healing* (Kingsway, 1979), re. Wilbourne Case.

John Macquarrie (ed.), *Principles of Christian Theology* (SCM Press, 1977). Especially sections on 'Selfhood' (pp. 74–83) and 'Soul' (pp. 362–3).

A. R. Peacocke, *God and the New Biology* (J. M. Dent, 1986).

W. H. Salter, *The Evidence of Psychical Research Concerning Survival* (Sidgwick & Jackson, 1961), re. the Chaffin Will Case.

Stephen H. Travis, *Christian Hope for the Future of Man* (IVP, 1980). Especially chapter 6, 'The Future Life'.

Keith Ward, *The Battle for the Soul* (Hodder & Stoughton, 1985). Especially chapter 2, 'The Elimination of Purpose from the Universe'.

Leslie Weatherhead, *Life Begins at Death* (Denholm House Press, 1970).

The quotation from Malcolm Muggeridge on pp. 86–7 is taken from *Muggeridge: the Biography*, Richard Ingrams (Harper Collins, 1995).

APPENDIX III

FOR FURTHER READING

R. T. France, *The Evidence for Jesus* (Hodder and Stoughton, 1986).

A. Godin (ed.), *Death and Presence (The Psychology of Death and the After-life)* (Lumen Vitae Press, Brussels, 1972).

John Houghton, *The Search for God: Can Science Help?* (Lion, 1995).

Dr Alison Morgan, *What Happens When We Die?* (Kingsway, 1995).

Gerald O'Collins, *Jesus Risen* (Darton, Longman & Todd, 1987).

John Polkinghorne, *Science and Providence* (SPCK, 1989).

John V. Taylor, *Kingdom Come* (SCM Press, 1989).

Stephen H. Travis, *Christian Hope and the Future of Man* (IVP, 1980).

Keith Ward, *The Battle for the Soul* (Hodder & Stoughton, 1985).

C. Zaleski, *Otherworld Journeys: Accounts of Near-Death Experience in Medieval and Modern Times* (Oxford University Press, 1987).